CW00493748

THE KRAKOW DIARY OF JULIUS FELDMAN

Quill

The Translator

William Brand has lectured at universities in the United States and Poland, and translated a number of books from Polish into English, including several memoirs of the Holocaust and the Second World War. Recently, he has cooperated with the Auschwitz-Birkenau Museum and translated the five-volume Auschwitz: Central Issues in the History of the Camp (2001). *He has also made several documentary films on Polish-Jewish relations. He lives today in Krakow, where he has been a resident for many years.*

THE KRAKOW DIARY
of Julius Feldman

Translated by William Brand

Published in Great Britain by
Quill Press
Woodlands, Main Street, Kirton,
Newark, Notts. NG22 9LP, UK

Published by Quill Press, April 2002

British Library Catalogue in Publication Data
A catalogue record for this book is available from the British Library

ISBN 0-9536280-8-6

Printed and bound by
Jellyfish Print Solutions, Swanmore

Cover montage: Julius Feldman aged 18, from the photograph used for his Ausweis *(work card), overlaid with the first page of his diary.*
Reverse cover: Julius Feldman as a small child.

INTRODUCTION

Written over a period of just two months in the spring of 1943, Julius Feldman's record, part memoir and part diary, brings to life the constant fears and desperate hopes, the daily grind and the appalling personal tragedies of life in the Krakow Ghetto in ways that only an eyewitness account written in the very heart of those events possibly could.

And this is no ordinary account, written as it was during the last and most turbulent days of the Krakow Ghetto's existence. With extraordinary courage and considerable personal initiative, Julek, as he was known, somehow found a way to carry on writing this diary following incarceration in the terrifying conditions of the Plaszow concentration camp, where discovery could quite easily have led to his death.

Assigned to the forced labour unit collecting, sorting and repairing furniture left behind by Jews interned at Plaszow or deported to extermination camps such as Auschwitz, each day Julek and his fellow prisoners would march out under the watchful eyes of German and Ukrainian guards to their working place in the former ghetto. There, in a secure place in the wall, Julek would hide the textbook in which he wrote.

Within its worn pages, he shares his life as it descends from normality into nightmare. Perhaps most poignant of all is his description of the loss of his family when they are rounded up for deportation: "My poor Father … held his hands out helplessly to show that he was going into the unknown, dressed in a summer coat and street shoes. Dear Janek wept terribly as he walked alone. Perhaps he met up with Mother somewhere because they were not far from each other. Oh, God! Who could say what awaited them, what new misery lay ahead as they walked into such a horrible winter completely unprepared?"

While questioning God and wondering what he has done to deserve his fate, somehow Julek remains stoical despite the pain. He was evidently careful to conceal certain information, too, in case of the diary's discovery by the Nazis: 'Mr. S.', and the kind 'Mrs. P.', for example, remain nameless. Nor does he ever discuss the means by which he was able to conceal the act of writing this diary.

Towards the end, he describes "facing a big decision which could be a matter of life or death." What this was, we will never know. On 11 April 1943, while seemingly in full flow, his diary ends abruptly, mid-sentence. We do not know what happened to Julek. Only one thing is certain; he did not survive the Holocaust.

After the war, while restoring the building where he had worked, Polish workers found his manuscript hidden in the wall. A small part of it was published in a local news magazine. Anda Goldschmied-Noworol, a cousin of Julek's who had returned to Krakow, was able to buy the manuscript and save it. She gave it to Julek's aunt, Renia Feldman, who took the manuscript to London and gave it to Julek's cousin, Oscar Feldman. It is thanks to him and to his widow, Gisela, who brought it to my attention, that this singular and remarkable document has now been published.

In order to remain as true as possible to the original Polish text, translator William Brand has avoided embellishing the style of the writing in places where phrasing may seem rough or awkward. Endnotes have been provided to facilitate the reader's understanding of its historical context, along with an excellent timeline of the Krakow Ghetto's existence compiled by Joseph Soski.

The diary of Julius Feldman is not a literary masterpiece, but rather, an account which reflects the circumstances of its production and can provide unique insights from one individual's precarious vantage point within the Holocaust. An invaluable source for historians of the Krakow Ghetto and for any student of the human impact of the 'Final Solution', this text brings us as close as any can to those tragic events.

Julius Feldman was born in Krakow on 24 December 1923. Almost certainly, at the time of his death, whether by bullet or gas, he was only 19 years old.

Stephen D Smith, MBE, PhD

In memory of

Julius Feldman

24.12.1923 – 1943-5 (date unknown)

and all the members of his family

who did not survive

CONTENTS

THE DIARY

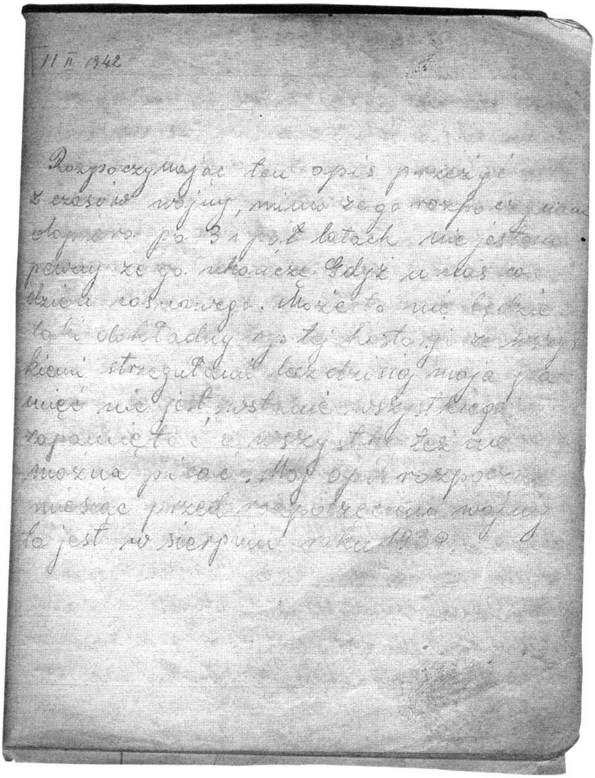

THE DIARY

11 February 1943[1]

Starting on this description of experiences from wartime, I have begun three and a half years late, and I am not sure that I will finish it since every day brings something new here. This might not be an exact sketch of the story with all the details, but my memory today is not capable of recalling everything. Nor is it possible to write everything. I shall begin my description a month before the start of the war, that is, in August 1939.

Personally, I have always been quite interested in newspapers, with their reports about politics and various other events. My father subscribed to *Naprzod* [*Forward*], a newspaper with a socialist orientation, and therefore I held the same views from the very beginning. Every day brought something new, whether it was vast armaments, or the murder of some politician, or again some sort of political or economic pact with one of the countries. All of this added up to the spectre of something ominous, something terrifying – 'War'. As for us, we did not really believe in this reality. We had our government, our press, and the speeches by our leaders who were so sure of themselves, in their strength and pride, that the possibility that Germany would attack the unified bloc of England, France and Poland over something as trivial as Gdansk never entered our heads. We turned out enthusiastically for the parades and various other ceremonies. We listened attentively to various radio programmes, talks or orchestras that were intended to reinforce our certainty and faith in the Polish army and the might of the Polish nation.

In those days, there were no Poles, Jews, Ukrainians and others who might hold differing views. Poland was everyone's fatherland. How lovely it all seemed! Until mobilization came. Even then, I did not realize. It was all a demonstration to the enemy of our strength. The return *en masse* from summer holidays and the buying up of foodstuffs all brought the beginning closer.

At home, things were somewhat grim. Despite the fact that everything was so cheap, our miserable earnings diminished so quickly that some days there was no money to buy bread in the morning. Not that it mattered – we were all wrapped up in politics. Then that terrible, mysterious thing happened. The war began, in the early morning of 1 September. Nothing like that had crossed our minds as we went to bed the evening before. I had made plans about how I would spend the day: swimming at the stadium in the morning and other pleasures in the afternoon. I was awakened by the echoes of a detonation. At first, I thought it was a storm. Then my mother got up, went to the window and noticed strange clouds of smoke in the sky and swarms of aeroplanes circling around like flies. We decided that it must be an exercise and that the aeroplanes must be the famed Polish *Los* model, which in any case I had never seen before. No one thought for a moment that it was the first air raid. We dressed unhurriedly. When I went out into the street, I heard the first rumours, the first apparently reliable news. This was no exercise, but real war. By word of mouth, reports spread that on Warszawska Street, or some other street, this or that building had been destroyed by bombs, that there was a fire at the airport, that fragments of shrapnel from the anti-aircraft artillery had fallen on Podgorze Square.[2] News of victory spread by word of mouth: ten aeroplanes had been shot down. No one had seen it, but everyone knew. Yet there was nothing new on the radio, only music and more music.

The first newspapers only appeared at noon, after the walls had been plastered with President Moscicki's[3] proclamation summoning the nation to defend itself against the eternal foe of civilization, the state of the Western Huns. What was the news in the papers? Victory! The Germans had been driven back everywhere. There were Polish aeroplanes over Berlin. France was attacking from the west. In general, all was well.

In the meantime, one air raid followed another. The radio broadcast some sort of odd signals which seemed to be a kind of secret code. Every so often there were instructions about how to defend against the Fifth Column[4] and spies. There was enemy eavesdropping everywhere. Two boys climbed onto the roof of a nearby house to watch the air raids. Someone saw them and in an instant, everyone knew and the police came. Who were those boys? Spies signalling the aeroplanes. They searched everywhere and finally came to our apartment, saying that we had been on the roof and that they wanted to arrest my father. After prolonged explanations, pleas and a pair of small mirrors thrown in as a gift, they left. How things had changed in a few days! And how quickly! We waited one day and then the next in constant anticipation of the decisive victory so grandly announced by the radio and newspapers.

Finally came that Sunday, that Sunday full of feverishness, full of nerves and full of joy. We were awakened at daybreak by the howling of the siren, and the alarm lasted for half the day without a break. People sat in their cellars and then went out into the street for news – only good news, for bad news did not exist. Then at noon, like a bolt from the blue, came joy, indescribable joy, and cheerfulness and smiles on every face. What was it? What had happened? England and France were fighting shoulder to shoulder with Poland. England and France had declared war on the Germans. We were no longer alone. The Western powers would finally do something.

A bomb hit the railway bridge not far away. Soldiers in the train crossing the bridge were wounded and killed. Everyone ran there with bandages, medication, or whatever they had to hand. My father and I were there, too. We hurried with shovels to fill in the bomb crater so that normal communication could resume. On every face you could see the desire to make sacrifices and to help our poor fatherland in its travails. That was true patriotism.

Towards evening, the first Silesian Line buses drove along the street carrying evacuees and the wives and children of officials from Katowice. What was going on? Victory on the front lines and people were beginning to flee. Something was wrong. Nobody knew what was happening.

THE DIARY

Monday brought mass flight, and a madness seized people. Whether or not this was the work of the 'Fifth Column', whose members were marched off to the police every so often, no one could say.

Government officials were being evacuated. The trains were unbearably overcrowded; everyone was trying feverishly to escape. On the streets, you could see little groups of people, then larger groups, and finally a whole phalanx of people hurrying along with their children – mothers with babies in prams or even held at their breasts. Everyone was fleeing. They were fleeing from the Germans – the Germans who cut off the ears, noses and hands of everyone they laid their hands on, or dug out their eyes, or generally did unimaginable things. We began to feel true fear. We started seeing acquaintances from town, wearing light clothing and carrying small travelling cases, walking along with no specific destination.

And then something changed. There was not a single Polish aeroplane to be seen. Where were we? And the soldiers were marching east. What was going on? Where were they going since the Germans were to the west? The Polish soldiers were supposedly marching towards Tarnow, and from there to the Carpathians where there was a threat from the south. Was that true? We believed that it was. We had to believe. The truth was: the Germans were advancing full tilt and we were fleeing.

The wave of refugees intensified on Tuesday morning. By then, the street we lived on looked deserted. My uncle, who lived nearby, came to talk things over. Should we leave or stay? We didn't want to leave, I don't know why. Perhaps we were short of cash, I can't say. In any case, I asked my uncle to take me along if he left with my cousin (Edek). The hours passed. We took our leave of Uncle Slomek who was passing our way from town with his wife and my cousin Frydka. We asked him to stay, to stay with us where it was safer than at his place (Uncle Slomek lived on the top floor of a five-storey block of flats). He could not make up his mind, but Aunt Anda pulled him away: "Come on, come on, Zelek (my father) can't say goodbye to his house." In the end, Uncle Slomek left us the keys to his shop and said, "If you can, look in some time and see what's going on there."[5] Almost everyone was leaving like them. We were terribly upset, and terribly downcast. What could we do?

And the radio! It kept reporting a victory here, a victory there, interspersed with constant appeals against spies, against the Fifth Column, and in general against all Germans. Uncle Szymek left without me. What could I do? Where could I hide? What could I do?

The streets were in turmoil again. Someone said the water had been poisoned. Alas! It was divine punishment! The rumours went on getting louder. Some guy ran down a nearby street shouting, "Don't drink the water! I've been poisoned!" There was tremendous confusion. People rushed to pour away all their supplies of water and to turn off the mains. I had drunk some water a moment earlier, so I drank glass after glass of milk as a purgative and took all possible preventive measures.

The streets were increasingly desolate; few neighbours or acquaintances remained. Now even the police were fleeing. What next? My father and I, the only men left, were in danger. We went down into the cellar to prepare a hiding place. We arranged the old straw, coal boxes and other junk to make a dark corner, which we padded as well as we could before bringing down supplies of food and water. No one could say how long we would have to sit there. We were terribly nervous. My father panicked and we rushed about like madmen.

The trains that had been fleeing east on both tracks stopped. No one knew what had happened, then it all ended gradually. After dinner, the city looked abandoned – a great void. A neighbour who had stayed behind told us she had heard from an officer that the Germans had been driven back 30 kilometres at the Bodzow forts.[6] How could that be? After all, they hadn't crossed the border yet. We believed this – what else could we do? Evening fell slowly. Out of curiosity, I tried lying down in our hiding place; it was very comfortable, except that it was too short.

We were exhausted and lay down to sleep in our clothes. At midnight, we were on our feet. What was going on? Powerful detonations broke the silence. We all ran down into the cellar. We wanted to get there, whether it would do any good or not. I began calculating. The Poles had surely blown up the bridges over the Vistula and intended to defend Krakow from the Podgorze and Krzemionki[7] sides. We were getting bored in the cellar. Regardless of my mother's pleas, I went back to lie down. Getting a good night's sleep was a wise move. And in the morning? We kept on waiting, but there was no one to be seen. We heard gunfire somewhere in the distance. The poor people who were left, and even the rich, ran through the streets towards the chocolate and alcohol factories, or the Kernel bakery, and then returned home with looted goods. I saw some of them carry off whole sacks of flour, bread or chocolate. When those articles ran out, they slyly loaded up with items which were of no use whatsoever to them. They did not even hesitate before eating a sort of yellowish fat used in making chocolate, which left them seriously ill afterwards. Anything was possible at that time.

While some people were saying that the Germans had already blown up the bridges and the railway station, others insisted that the Polish troops had withdrawn so the French could take up their positions. Their army was in the city and we gradually accustomed ourselves to that mood.

Slowly, we stopped believing the awful tales about the Germans. Weren't they people, too? I went out to the street corner. Now what? I suddenly noticed three motorcycles ridden by soldiers, approaching at full speed from the direction of Wieliczka.[8] Who were they? Nobody knew. Their helmets looked German, but they had a tricolour insignia on them. So the French really must be here! Overjoyed, I ran home to describe what I had seen. My great happiness ended quickly, however, because it turned out that those soldiers were our enemies. Yet our political gossip went on as before. Our troops had surely withdrawn from the city to prevent the destruction of its historical monuments; they would probably recapture it after striking at the enemy flank. In the meantime, the Germans had in fact not only entered Krakow, but were already advancing beyond the city.

This was the first time I had seen strong troops. They looked more than strong – they looked downright powerful. Motorized units were heading eastward down the street at full speed. It was all so new for us.

Groups of Polish soldiers began walking past in the afternoon, but they were under German escort and carried their rifles with the barrels pointing downwards. God, had we expected to see this? We gave them whatever we had left and their escorts turned a blind eye. Evening came and my father told me about the news on the radio. Everything was fine, the Germans had indeed gained some territory, but at a very high price. We knew how true that was. I went onto the balcony after supper – just for a moment. And then, for some reason, I began to cry, I don't know why. The tears simply came when I thought about what had happened. We had lost, we had been defeated. I hardly knew then how long we would suffer and be under the yoke. Yet we believed that everything would change soon.

From that moment, I cannot recall precisely what happened and in what order. I shall therefore recount it in general terms.

I know that only one page of the *Kurier Codzienny* [*Daily Courier*] came out the following day. It included short reports on how the city had capitulated and the vice-mayor had handed over the keys. Our life under foreign rule was beginning. An order was issued that life should continue as normal. The trams began running again, shops were made to open, but it was forbidden to go anywhere after nine o'clock.

Since my father had the key to my uncle's shop, he had to go there every morning to open it. Out of curiosity, I resumed going round to the sites of bombed-out buildings and surveying for the first time the effects of the war. Something resembling normal life began again. My father was summoned for labour at the airport and he became the foreman in charge of glazing work there.

On one of the first days when he was at work, two soldiers called on us at noon on the pretext of searching for weapons. They looked everywhere, rapped on the walls and stole what they could. My mother and I were alone and could do nothing. They were common thieves sent by someone (a 'good friend') to our address. It was only when they had left, taking all our valuables, that we realised we had been set up. When my father returned, he accused us of having been careless and neglectful. Yet what could we have done? We soon forgot about it. New regulations kept coming out.

My mother and I went to the shop to sell off the merchandise, and kept a careful eye on things. In the meantime, the war in our land was coming to an end, except in Warsaw, Modlin and the Hel Peninsula.[9] Poland was being defeated.

The Russians were entering eastern Poland.[10] What had happened? They had made a deal with the Germans: it was another riddle.

We took on great responsibilities towards Uncle Slomek, in his shop, his warehouse, and his apartment on Dietla Street.[11] Relatives moved in there who had been resettled from Ostrava in Moravia.[12] They joined the maid in stealing whatever they could, we had no way of knowing. It was only later, with the help of the Sternbergs and Aunt Renia, that we started moving things to the warehouse. But it was all for nothing: I can see as I write these words today how all our efforts went to waste.

Now to personal matters. As I mentioned, I was working in the shop. At the end of September, however, after registration for secondary school in the *gimnazjum* [high school] No. IV building, I began preparing for school.

So far, only a few anti-Jewish regulations had come out:[13] Jews were forbidden to have more than 2,000 *zloty* or to engage in politics, and their shops had to be marked with the star of Zion.[14]

THE DIARY

I have completely forgotten to write that the wave of refugees gradually returned. People who had been at the other end of Poland returned full of experiences and adventures. Among the many acquaintances who came back were Uncle Szymek and Edek.

At some point in October, they finally re-opened our school and work began. After a speech by our old principal, everyone cried. He appealed to us to redouble our efforts, to work and learn so that we could pick ourselves back up. We went to the Sobieski *gimnazjum* in the afternoon, since our school had been taken over by the army. There were some pupils as well as teachers missing, but it all held together somehow and we had our lessons. But school life with all its emotions, as it was before the war, never returned. We were depressed by the turn of fate, and only individuals unable to appreciate the seriousness of the moment behaved badly. I was the only Jew in my class, but I did not feel like a stranger among my old classmates of previous years. However, some of the new boys who did not know me did things to hurt and annoy me. How I wished that they too would show a little sense, that their eyes could be opened so they could see what was going on in my heart. Did the fact that I was a Jew prevent me from being their friend? Did I love my fatherland, where I had been raised and educated, any differently from them? Unfortunately, they could not understand. Perhaps they realise today. In any case, our school year was brief – it ended around 6 November. I don't know why, but the German police called on the Principal during lessons that day and delivered an order closing the school. We left, talking about what had happened. We thought it was a preventive measure connected with the 11 November holiday, but we never went to school again. Catholics[15] were allowed to enrol in vocational schools half a year or so later, but my education was over.[16] Why? Because I was a Jew. "Because," as my father put it, "a Jewish mother gave birth to me." Therein lay my guilt.

I had been deprived of something hard to define, something that cannot so easily be expressed.

I began working regularly in the shop. At nine o'clock every morning, I went into town taking the key. My only co-worker was Fredi Hoffmann. We got used to each other, got along well, and became friends. It seems strange to put it this way, but I had my first job, my first entry into the world of people with duties and responsibilities. So November passed. More and more unpleasantness and worries. The word 'Jew' came out into the light of day. Jewish shops came under German commissars[17] and administrators, or were even requisitioned outright.

Aunt Anda wrote from Lwow[18] that she intended to come to Krakow. That would be a good thing, since at times we did not know what to do to avoid making a mistake.

We also expected a commissar in the shop; there was nothing we could do about it. My father continued working at the airport and life was not too bad for him there. He had also managed to get on the good side of various Germans who took care of him. There were even times when he repeated what they told him about the situation. Not that it mattered.

My mother stayed at home with Janek and only looked in on the business from time to time.

We heard various items of news and expected the war to end soon. The first winter of the war was beginning; it was severe and frosty, but it did not yet affect us. Via various trustworthy and reliable people, we sent winter things to Lwow, where it now seemed that my aunt and uncle were going to remain. Not everything reached them. That, too, was the way things had to be.

With the help of a friend, I began trying to make up the school work from the fourth class at home. We forged ahead together. I thought then that I would be able to pass my exams if the war came to a sudden end. Unfortunately, it did not.

In December, we had to surrender our radio,[19] the only source of news. We turned in our Philips set, and Uncle Slomka's ...

Prices kept going up. In general, things were getting worse. Regulations came out requiring Jews to wear an armband ten centimetres wide, with a blue Star of David, on their right sleeve.[20] What would that look like? We could not accept it. I don't remember when the deadline passed, but I did not put one on; in fact, I did not wear one for about two weeks. On my way into town by tram, I got my first look at a Jew wearing that symbol. What a sight! I was stunned. Anybody who felt like it could pick us out and harass us. We were like those medieval Jews marked with a yellow patch and this was supposed to be the civilized Twentieth Century! But that was nothing. Whenever any work needed doing – for the army or administration – it became the accepted practice for Jews to be rounded up everywhere on the streets, and they were the ones who had the honour of labouring. Various army trucks drove around giving free rides to workers. The situation made us very cunning. At the first distant sign of something suspicious, the street became empty – no Jews. They were all indoors; everyone hid who was able to do so. Apart from this, there were roving requisition commissions that went from one building to another confiscating all the best furniture. And in addition, they helped themselves to silver, crystal and even clothing at the same time.

All of this, however, is in the past as I write these words. Today, such things are not even worth mentioning, but back then life had its emotions. Many songs were composed about current events, such as *I'll Be Coming on Horseback*, and others. In general, we gradually got used to everything.

We had very little news from the outside world: nothing certain, only speculation. France would strike at the Siegfried Line[21] in the spring, of that we were certain. If that meant a longer war, so be it. We were great optimists. Thus, winter passed and spring came.

Things got worse and worse for my father at the airport, and all because he was Jewish. There were so many complaints from the Catholics that my father was even summoned to Pomorska Street[22] for clarification, but everything turned out well. Yet the pressure increased until he and the rest of the Jews employed there were dismissed in

March or April – I cannot remember precisely when. He received a very positive letter of reference for his work.

Our situation grew worse. Things were also deteriorating at the shop. We had to sell our merchandise and enter it in the account books, but any German firm could requisition the best goods if it wanted to. So, for instance, the German firm Hoffmann took all the picture frames.

Life dragged on monotonously from day to day. Nor was there anything new at home. After Agnysia[23] left to get married, having been with us for fourteen years, my mother had to do everything herself in the apartment and around the building. In general, my beloved mother was such a hard worker that she had time for everything.

My father decided to re-open his glass-polishing shop, since there was nothing else to do. He made pocket and bathroom mirrors which I sold in the shop. There was no real work to be done except trying to keep busy, which was hardly profitable. But there was no alternative; it was a matter of staying in practice.

There were new regulations and restrictions all the time. In March, all Jews aged between 16 and 60 had to register. This was supposed to be the first step towards compulsory labour. An *Arbeitsamt* would be opened on Podbrzezie Street[24] and we would all be subject to it. My father and I registered as skilled workers, father as a master craftsman and I as an apprentice. I registered at the shop with the Social Insurance Office so that I would be assured of work. Somehow, life went on.

Spring slowly approached and our predictions proved wrong. We had said that the higher the sun, the closer Sikorski[25] came. Instead, the Germans attacked Denmark and

Norway, defeating those countries after shorter or longer campaigns. We descended from patriotic optimism into depression: deeper and deeper pessimism. The tension grew worse when the strike against France through Holland and Belgium came. No one knew how it would turn out or who would be defeated. In any case, England could help instead of watching other countries bloody each other. Anything could happen. In the meantime, the Germans advanced. I was just leaving the warehouse with Fredi to go to the shop when a special edition came out: Paris had fallen and the French Government had fled south. This capitulation, the various changes and the flight of various politicians were like a cold shower for us. However, when England refused to cave in under the blow, announcing that the French had betrayed them and they would fight on in the name of freedom, our uncertainty was somehow eased.

We began having more to do. A German commissar named Floder finally came to the shop, and we had to turn everything over to him and give him an accounting. The money went to the *Treuhandstelle* [Trust Office]. I only worked two more weeks for him. He brought in new people in order to remove me and my mother. He only ordered merchandise from my father at the polishing shop. I then worked with my father and registered at home with the Social Insurance Office.

Scant news reached us from my aunt in Lwow. People who had heard things or been there said various sorts of things. In any case, people said at the time that it was better where we were, and that was why some people there wanted to return.

THE DIARY

The beginning of summer saw the first assignments of us Jews to forced labour: roundups began. Since we did not live in Kazimierz, we were at less risk. Nevertheless, no one felt secure. Nor was I passed over. I received a summons to present myself and prepare to depart – to Debica,[26] I believe. In general, many positions were being created for forced labour, building dykes along the Vistula in Pychowice or Koszczy,[27] or in the lime-pits and brickyards. My father somehow managed to arrange for me to stay in Krakow with an assignment to work in the municipal gardens, instead of being sent away. It was very pleasant work, although it was also quite exhausting. I still have many more or less agreeable memories of it and I got to know many young men and women acquaintances. It seems that I worked there for two months, although I cannot remember precisely. I left there through a strange twist of fate. When they were making up the files at the *Arbeitsamt*, I managed to convince them that I worked with my father, without mentioning my real work assignment.

In the meantime, the first deportations began. In order to stay in Krakow, you had to submit a petition requesting permission. Those who were accepted received an *Ausweis* [permit][28] but those who were rejected had to present themselves for deportation, with a 25-kilogramme parcel. Things worked out well somehow and my father was among the first to receive an *Ausweis*. My mother, brother and I got ours some two weeks later.

Hardly anything new happened from then until late autumn; the war dragged on. People traded rumours and said various things. Some said one thing, and some another. We went to Uncle Szymek's in the evenings to play cards or chess. We also visited Sieprawski's often. Corruption in the deportations was revealed, in which many people were involved. Because of this, everything was checked again. Every holder of an *Ausweis* had to submit a special *Fragebogen* or questionnaire form.

A new deportation operation began. In the meantime, I spent several days working outside of Krakow at the train station in Brzezie,[29] where my father was doing some glazing.

People without any Ausweis kept being rounded up. They had to disappear from Krakow. Uncle Szymek and his family went to Borek.[30] Everything went on this way until, I believe, 8 December. On that day, we received notification that our further residence in Krakow was invalid, and that we should report to Lubicz Street[31] with 25-kilogramme parcels. That was the first mishap, the first misfortune, and it struck us like a bolt of lightning. My parents' health took a turn for the worse that day. They both looked many years older. I myself cannot say how we coped. I know that my father and mother went to Borek. Along with the workers, I packed hastily. We took the better things, such as merchandise and tools, to Mr. S.

in Zablocie.[32] Everyone stole what they could: we lost a lot of things that way. Upstairs in the apartment, it was even worse, in even greater disorder. Everyone was packing blindly, ordering others around and stealing. We stored two crates full of various items at our neighbours' and other smaller things as well. Father came back from Borek to say that everything was ready and we went there in the *Zuzug*.[33] Father had come from there with a married couple, with whom we were to exchange apartments. In return for our three-room apartment, they gave us something like workshop premises, which were practically unusable, but there was nothing we could do and no choice since nothing else was vacant in Borek.

That night, we did not sleep at home, but rather at our neighbour's across the hall. We were afraid of being discovered. In the morning, our employees took some of our furniture to 5 Tarnowskiego Street[34] where we had a basement. We began transporting our belongings to that 'factory', as we called it. We could not even live there at first because it had no windows. Our employee, Buchsbaum, made some for us. My father and Janek slept at Aunt Lorka's, I slept at Mrs. Goldstein's on Podgorze Square and my mother stayed with someone on Kingi St.

In the meantime, those people moved into our apartment: Mr. Fijol, a sergeant in the Polish army who pretended to be a major in order to impress us (a big drunk) and his mistress, a native of Borek named Gorska, with her sons (I will have a lot more to write about these good Poles later). In the meantime, we were homeless.

One day in December, when I was still sleeping at Mrs. G.'s, there was a roundup in Podgorze in the morning and everything happened on the Square, almost under our windows. We were very fortunate that they barely set foot in our building. Otherwise, I would have been caught which was the last thing I needed. We were getting used to this sort of thing: it was nothing in comparison to what we are living through now. After that incident, I went to Borek, for I no longer felt safe. We lived miserably until there were windows in the factory to keep the weather out. The time came to move in there. We once again had to move the things we needed, including beds and clothing, and the wagon was stopped by the Polish police. We would have lost everything, since it was forbidden to transport anything out of Krakow. We got out of it somehow, saying that the goods were not Jewish, but belonged to that Fijol.

And so we moved into the factory on Kopernika Street in Borek. That might seem fine, but within a week we had to start looking for a real apartment and not that workshop, since no one could bear the cold and frost there. I could write a lot about that. In any case, the best we could do was to find a room rented out in Lagiewniki[35] by someone named Trotiner. Once again, we were all together in a warm apartment.

In the meantime, Fijol and Mrs. Gorska began making themselves at home in our place on Kingi Street. He was drunk every day and held all sorts of wild parties, destroying everything in the apartment, smashing the windows, breaking the water closet and so on. They were the sort of people who had never lived in an apartment like that before and did not know how to behave.

A pass was required to go into town from Borek. We were trying to figure out whether to put our building under the administration of a commissar, or what to do. We had made a big mistake at the beginning by liquidating the glass-polishing shop. We should have done what other people did, which was to live in Borek and commute to their business. We, on the other hand, lost everything.

In the meantime, there was work shovelling snow in Krakow. You were supposed to work for twelve days and you got a stamp on the back of your *Ausweis*.[36] I found someone for whom I got ten stamps, thus earning 80 *zloty*. That was attractive for me. The work was in two shifts, from 7:00 to 13:00 and from 14:00 to 20:00. I went there every afternoon and came home nine hours later, not wearing a Jewish armband. I also worked in Borek on several occasions, either for myself or for my father.

Once, when my mother was in Podgorze, she found Mrs. Gorska's son and two other men in our glass workshop. She could not understand how they had got in since she was carrying the key. When she asked them what they were doing there, they replied that they wanted to buy the glass, which they were in the process of sorting. She simply did not know what to do, or from whom they wanted to buy the glass. We had no idea what was going on. Naturally, they had used a key made by Mr. Fijol or Mrs. Gorska to get in, and it was either Fijol or Gorska who was selling the glass. My mother left in despair and told the whole story to our neighbour, Mr. Zeberka, who went to see an acquaintance of his, a police detective (I cannot recall his name – perhaps I will later). The detective wrote a whole report on how it had been discovered and passed the matter on to the Criminal Division of the police. First, he put a seal on the workshop door to prevent further theft. We felt relieved when we heard this. We thought that everything would turn out well, but it took a completely different turn. As we discovered, those two men were Germans and when they learned our whole story from Fijol, they went to inform the *Treuhandstelle* that our furniture was in storage on Tarnowskiego Street. That was all it took. They then went there and ordered the superintendent, Mrs. Wojtowicz, to open the basement. They took everything. They must have taken it all somewhere on Retoryka Street[37] since the cart driver was from Cmentarna Street (I forget his name). All this was nothing because the story would go on for months. We got used to the loss because we understood that the furniture meant nothing to us, but we would make it up with interest if the war ended well.

In the meantime, things moved slowly forward with the police Criminal Division. My mother and Janek were called in for questioning several times. The commissar who was running everything was a bad man to begin with and had been worked on by those German gentlemen. He wanted to manage the investigation in such a way that we, and not they, would be accused. The case dragged on. My father was finally called in for questioning and he presented matters in the proper way, explaining how people who had been caught red-handed were trying to absolve themselves and shift the blame to us. In any case, I have no idea whether those people were charged, or what they were charged with. The only thing that happened was that the key to the workshop was sent on to the Prosecutor's office. We tried to get it back through our lawyer. The Prosecutor's office returned it to the police, saying that since they had not been the ones who had taken it, they could not release it. All of our efforts came to nothing. We wanted to rent the glazier's workshop to our employee Wladyslaw and later to a glazier who had been resettled from Poznan, but nothing worked out. The key made its way from the police back to the *Treuhandstelle*, which again ordered that the workshop should be liquidated, and so on. But I will write about this later. In the meantime, we were living in Lagiewniki.

In Krakow, they began issuing the identification card known as the *Kennkarte*.[38] Father tried to get such cards for us and used his connections with the craftsmen. President Lipner[39] was very helpful. Our application was finally accepted and around 10 March we were due to pick up the identification cards, which were waiting for us. My father, mother, and I went into town, to the office on Lubicz Street.[40] Mother had to go back home to get their marriage licence, which took all day. I received my *Kennkarte* immediately upon paying 20 *zloty*. I showed the card proudly to my uncle and Edek in Borek. (We did not know then that our troubles were far from over, and that all of us, along with those identity cards, had some difficult times ahead.)

I have forgotten to write that a ghetto was being set up in Krakow. There were to be two parts, Ghetto A and Ghetto B. Since Kingi Street was in sector B, we expected to move back into our apartment. Mrs. Gorska had been forced to move out a month earlier. I should add one last thing about Mrs. Gorska. When she moved back to Borek, she sold our hand-cart without our knowledge. Father later came across it at Zajac the ironmonger's on Kalwaryjska Street.[41] It was nothing; it made no difference to us.

The time for resettlement to the ghetto was approaching. Catholics were supposed to move out of both sectors A and B and the Jews were supposed to move in by a certain deadline. I think it was 20 March. We prepared to leave Lagiewniki. I have many memories of life in Borek, such as various little scandals, transactions, and the passionate collecting and trading of postage stamps with my friends. We moved to Krakow at exactly the right time. Janek and I went with the cart while our mother and father finished packing. Thus we arrived and moved back into our old apartment. There was hardly any furniture left and we lived with bare walls. There were only a few other neighbours in the whole street. We waited for future developments.

The conquest of Yugoslavia and Greece by the Germans had a very pessimistic effect on us. In general, the war had gone on for so long and we were so longing for it to end. Every Sunday, I went to see my cousin and friends in Borek. I went without a pass or an armband, which was a big risk, but then again I did not look so strikingly Jewish. The Zebereks were the only other family living in the whole street. We did not really have permission to live in Ghetto B, but only to live where everyone else lived in Ghetto A. Yet no such regulations had ever been issued. On the contrary, it was always referred to as Sector B of the Jewish residential district. Then a regulation came out stating that in order to prevent recurring thefts in vacant buildings, the owners or *concierges* should move back in – without specifying whether these owners were Catholics or Jews. We used that regulation to justify the fact that we lived there. At city hall, in the Jewish community and at the *Arbeitsamt* where we registered each month, our Kingi Street address was listed. They knew about us everywhere.

My mother engaged in a bit of commerce. Acquaintances came from the ghetto to buy milk or other things. Inevitably, someone informed on us and we were caught. They confiscated all the village women's milk and found three kilogrammes of meat at our place. Mother carelessly said that she had bought it from Mrs. H. across the way and they went to her place and found another ten kilogrammes. I had to carry it all to the police station on Zamoyskiego Street[42] where they wrote up a report about how we had been caught trading in contraband goods. This led to a long story. In the end, we had to pay a fine of something like 100 *zloty*. Our neighbour, Mrs. H., also paid a fine, and was understandably enraged with us for a while.

I have forgotten to mention that the Jewish district – it was forbidden to call it a ghetto – was closed off. Polish police stood at the gates checking passes, whether they were police passes or the *Passiererlaubnis*[43] kind issued by the *Arbeitsamt*. The *Passiererlaubnis* was stamped on the *Kennkarte* and prolonged for a month at a time. The *Kennkarte* was initially prolonged at the main *Arbeitsamt* on Lubicz Street and, after the closing of the ghetto, at the *Nebenstelle*[44] on Jozefinska Street. I had an assignment to work with my father and, as a construction glazier, I too had one of those passes.

It now occurs to me that I have forgotten to mention the news that we had from Aunt Anda. We learned that half a year earlier they had been deported from Lwow to somewhere in the vicinity of Kazan,[45] and this was the reason that we had heard nothing from them. We do not know exactly what happened to them afterwards.

Floder was running the shop as he pleased. He liquidated our absent uncle's business in the following way: he stated that the merchandise was of no substantial value and that there was no profit to be made from continuing to sell it. Then he purchased the whole business in his own name at a price that he set himself and became the legal owner. He also continued to act as commissar for the whole glazing trade and liquidated all the Jewish businesses one by one. He set up his own glazier's shop at a warehouse in Grodek,[46] using machines that he took from other people.

In the meantime, war broke out with Russia. We had been wondering for some time about the meaning of the enormous concentrations of German troops. Right up until the outbreak, the rumours had been contradicted by all the articles in the newspapers about the strengthening of friendly relations, dating back to Molotov's memorable visit to Berlin.

On that memorable Sunday, 22 June 1941, I went to Borek after dinner as usual. From early morning people had been murmuring and the atmosphere around us was heavy. As I walked hurriedly along the railway tracks through Krzemionki, one impressive-looking troop train after another passed. I wanted to tell my acquaintances in Borek the news as soon as possible. As I approached the houses, I could see that posters were up everywhere proclaiming that a total blackout had been ordered with immediate effect. My forebodings, which I had been sensing since morning, had come true. When I got there, everyone knew the secret that I had wanted to bring them as news.

On our usual walk through the meadows in Borek, we kept scanning the sky for Russian aeroplanes. As we walked along the road in the evening, somebody said that an *Extrablat*, an extra edition of the newspaper, had come out. Everyone was rushing feverishly towards the city and indeed, a special edition had been published with the grand headline 'The Reasons for Moscow's Betrayal.' How could it have happened? We had been unprepared until the last moment, and now what a bombshell! We drew a lot of conclusions from those times. Our interest in the newspapers increased considerably as well, but we also had more to do with regard to our own affairs.

As I have mentioned, the *Treuhandstelle* had turned our glazier's shop over to the liquidator so that he could wrap matters up. He also had the keys. It seemed as if everything was going to proceed as we wanted, and that he would sell the whole glazier's shop to a certain deportee from Poznan (an acquaintance of ours), whom I mentioned earlier. As luck would have it, however, the whole affair turned out badly for us. Mr. Floder butted in and decided to liquidate it himself. One day, a car pulled up at our address on Kingi Street. Floder, accompanied by a German policeman, demanded that we hand over the keys and the shop. We replied that we did not have the keys, the liquidator had them. He did not believe us, but what could he do? He believed that we had brought in the liquidator, and that the liquidator was acting in our interests. There was nothing they could do in the end, so the policeman asked on what basis we were living there. When my father showed him all the papers, the policeman ordered Father to go to Franciszkanska Street[47] the following day so that things could be checked. Then they left.

I do not recall the exact date, but my father went there in the morning. Mother sensed something and was very upset. We paced back and forth the whole time and mother lit candles for father's safe return. But there was no sign of him. One hour passed, then a second and a third, and there was no one in sight. We sent Janek to Mr. S. on Jozefa Street to make sure that Father wasn't there, but of course he wasn't. Something had happened and we were terribly downcast. Mother kept lamenting that he had surely been arrested. She did not know what to do. Liza F. wanted to notify the *Ordnungsdienst*[48] to see if they knew anything. Everyone tried to comfort us, and among others, Mrs. G. was helpful in all possible ways. Finally, mother and I went into town (she did not have a pass), to Franciszkanska Street to try to find out what was going on. They told us that they did not know anything. Where should we go? To Pomorska Street? I could not believe that things would have gone that far. He was not guilty of anything serious enough for the Gestapo to be involved. In the end, we went to Floder's in Grodek. He might know something or be able to give us some advice or help. After all, he had never been hostile; he had always regarded father as a human being. He was not there, so we waited for him. We told the whole story to Mr. Fischler, who was very anxious. He said that someone, apparently it was Ludwik, had reported seeing Father going somewhere accompanied by a policeman. That was enough for us. We wanted to find Fredi to see if he knew anything. In the meantime, however, Mr. Floder arrived.

Mother asked him what she should do, whether he knew anything and whether he could phone somewhere or ask someone. He politely refused, explaining that he could not become involved in this matter. We returned home in despair. Mother would not eat anything and cried all the time. We spent a sleepless night continually hoping that he might come home. By morning, nothing had happened. Mother went back to town with Janek. She went to Franciszkanska Street, Szlak[49] and even to Pomorska Street, where they did not want to let her in (Jews were not allowed there). Everywhere, the result was the same. No one knew anything. I stayed alone at home, waiting. Suddenly, a German policeman rode up to the door on a motorcycle. I thought he had come for me. I broke out in a cold sweat and walked out to meet him. He asked me if there was only one family living in the building and if they were the superintendents. I answered yes in a natural way and he rode off. I wondered what that could have meant and whether it was connected with father's case. Mother came back empty-handed. Yet it seems that Mrs. G. came with the news that a man had told her he had shared a *dorozke*[50] from the town to the ghetto with father, and that father had gone to the OD.[51] I ran quickly to the ghetto to check this information and, as if by some miracle, father was there. He was just getting ready to leave when I came running up. That was the first time I could remember that we kissed each other with so much feeling. We walked home joyfully. The happiness that we all felt is beyond description. We did not know whether to dance or jump up and down in delight. We put father to bed immediately and after washing and changing his clothes, he began telling us what it had really been like. He had gone to Franciszkanska Street and they ordered him to wait over five hours until a clerk came. At last, the clerk arrived. After writing his report, he did not know what to do about the whole matter so he sent father to Pomorska Street under the escort of a German policeman. This guard behaved very badly along the way, telling father to run or walk faster, which was hard for him to do at his age. Once there, the guard turned him over to the sentry. He received several blows across the face and a couple of kicks. They finally handed him over to Mr. K., the clerk for Jewish affairs. In the corridor, he met a Jew, Mr.S., who told him that it was forbidden to talk to him, all the more so as he was under arrest. After listening to the whole affair, the clerk called the OD. Pacanowe M.[52] answered the telephone and apparently said that we were living on Kingi Street legally, that everyone knew us and we were registered as living there (we learned all this several days later). Then he called the Jewish community (I don't know what they told him). In any case, since it was already evening they sent Father to Montelupich prison.[53]

The next day, he was taken back to Pomorska Street. Mr. Spira had been there in the meantime, and Mr. K. had given him father's *Kennkarte* together with other orders. They gave father a letter in place of his pass and a letter to the OD saying a suitable apartment was to be found in the ghetto within 24 hours, and that we were to be moved there. Father went by *dorozke* to the OD with the aforementioned man to get his *Kennkarte*, and that was where I found him. That was the end of father's imprisonment.

We had to move. They found us a nice room at 11 Benedykta Street[54] and we moved in. The Zebereks, who stayed behind, had a lot more trouble on that account, but that's a long story and does not belong in my memoir. Thus we began living in the ghetto. Unfortunately, we did not know what it would be like and what lay in store for us. In any case, we were happy that things turned out as they did and that we got as good an apartment as we did at a time when the housing shortage was getting worse: people were starting to move in from the vicinity and the rule was to assign three people for each window in a room, regardless of the room's size. It was only the beginning. Mr. Markowski, the owner of a glazier's shop, bought what was left of our shop and the glazing machines from the *Treuhandstelle*. I don't know what became of him or why he did this; he did not behave in any particular way toward us. We had no benefit from it. That was the end of our glazier's shop.

I carried various odds and ends, which were hardly worth anything, to the ghetto, where Father rented a tiny shop from Mr. Übersfeld. There, we put whatever we had saved.

A chauffeur who worked for the Germans moved into our apartment on Kingi Street. He was a very suspicious character and began running things as if he already owned the place. We transported things until we were ready to drop. Jewish painters were working in the workshop, making road signs. Father had recommended them. I forgot to say that our building had been under the administration of a commissar for some time. It did not matter. That was how things were until the end of winter. Our conditions in the ghetto could have been worse. I went with Father to Kingi Street every morning to buy milk, bread or meat from village women we knew. Thus the second year of the war passed and winter set in – the worst winter of the war. We could tell from the military communiqués that the Germans were thousands of kilometres deep in Russian territory and were now contending with the harsh winter and the attacking enemy. Our optimism was undimmed; on the contrary, the entry of America into the war on 8 December shored it up considerably. We believed the war would end in the spring after all. Various predictions by rabbis and saints, as well as astronomical calculations, were current. Such rumours were the order of the day.

Life in the ghetto worsened by the day. We sold things to buy food. The overcrowding was worse and worse. Then, sometime in December, we had to turn in all our fur.[55] This was an operation on a large scale. The penalty for possessing fur after the deadline was death, so it was no trivial matter. I think it was a Saturday. As usual, I went to Kingi Street in the morning. I was walking along the street and I could tell that there was an unusual commotion. Polish police were milling around everywhere; it was forbidden to leave the ghetto and people were asking each other what was going on. Then for the first time I heard that all fur, skis and ski boots larger than size 41 had to be turned in by eight o'clock in the evening. I went home quickly to discuss what we should do. Trucks with loudspeakers were driving up and down the streets announcing the regulations. At every step I heard "penalty of death, penalty of death". People were seized with panic and even those who wanted to hide something handed it over in their fear. I packed up Father's fur coat and Mother's collar. . . .

Everyone hurried to the Jewish Community building where they were collecting those items and a queue some 500 metres long formed. Everyone wanted to be first and hand in their fur on time. They received numbers as they waited so they would have something to show, just in case. We had very little to hand in, so we borrowed some merchandise from Uncle Szymek. On the streets, people were tearing up expensive furs. Fortunes were going to waste. What a sight it was! Terrible crowding in the queue, numb feet; you stood there for hours but what could you do? Everybody was pushing forward to give in their property as quickly as possible …

There was supposed to be a search the next day. Indeed, no one was allowed out on the streets from early morning. Trucks kept driving around announcing the deadline and what was supposed to be handed in. People were seized by indescribable panic. They lost their heads and hastily handed in everything connected with ski equipment. How foolish it all was! After an hour or so, the Gestapo began blocking off all the streets one by one and searching particular apartments. Everything went fine at our place. When they walked in, they could see that everything had been tidied up so they left immediately without looking for anything. Elsewhere, there were cases of beating and theft. In general, however, it all passed peacefully. In the whole ghetto, there were only something like two cases of the death penalty. The confiscated fur lay around for weeks in the warehouses, in some cases, until some use was made of it. After that incident, life went back to normal.

Work shovelling snow began on 1 January. It was required to go to work every Sunday. I cannot even remember where or how often I worked, or whether it was for myself or for Father. It was hard work. You had to go to the *Arbeitsamt* where you handed over your *Kennkarte* to be stamped, then to Grzegorzecka Street[56] for equipment, and then to the work site with someone designated by city hall. As in the previous year, many memorable things happened. The way it finally turned out is that people holding a *Passiererlaubnis* had to do this work only once in order to prolong their *Kennkarte*, but those who did not have a *Passiererlaubnis* had to work day in and day out. There was a lot of work at various military or private institutions: more on that subject later.

From then until June, nothing really important happened. The painters stopped working on Kingi Street. The new master upstairs, who worked in propaganda and acted as if he owned the place, wanted to have a garage close to where he lived, so he convinced his superiors to convert our glazier's workshop into a garage. They were supposed to take out the windows and make a door for him to drive in. In general, he made himself at home. On one occasion, his wife chased Father away, shouting that it was no longer his place, that we would never return. (She later apologized, but we were well aware of what she thought.) The conversion never took place and the commissar rented the shop to a certain Aryan firm that produced chemical items. They adapted the whole shop to their needs and began production. We stopped going there at that point because we had no business there. People worked wherever they could, for firms or privately, and I took any sort of job when Father could not. Among other things, we converted shop windows and used them to do glazing work around the ghetto. In general, it was a relatively calm period. Political interest slackened because the predictions about the end of the war had yet again failed to come true. We continued to live relatively comfortably on Benedykta Street. My friends visited and we spent our free time together. When the weather turned warmer, we walked around the ghetto or climbed the bit of Krzemionek that was inside the walls. We gazed jealously on the Catholics, who were free to walk all over Krakow. I made many friends in this period, both boys and girls, and have fond memories of moments such as the walks we had together.

I forgot to mention that for almost a year Jews had been forbidden to travel on trams. First, we were confined to a separate compartment and finally banned entirely. This prohibition was even extended to horse-drawn *dorozki* and other vehicles. We gradually got used to walking and even stopped minding.

In the spring, camps were created in Plaszow and Prokocim[57] for Jews from nearby small towns who were brought here to do various sorts of railway work. These were very poor people; every Sunday they came to the ghetto and begged for help in the streets, and people gave what they could. In general, expenses were rising markedly, but there was nothing to be done and those who could, gave something. And then came

June, a memorable month for every Jew in Krakow. That was when the first deportation took place. I will describe what it was like. I do not remember the date, but can still tell the story.

It began on a Saturday. There had been tension in the ghetto for several weeks. Something was hanging in the air and we expected something. Everybody was looking for a job so as to be as secure as possible. On that Saturday, I went out as usual for a walk through the streets with my friends and did not suspect anything. And then we learned that the ghetto had been surrounded by the *Sonderdienst.*[58] It was impossible to tell what it all meant, so I did not return home immediately, but waited until evening. When I got home, I hardly recognized our room. A woman who had been forced to move from Prokocim was there, along with her daughter. I should add that the same Saturday was the deadline for all the Jews in the vicinity to move to the ghetto. So our apartment looked as if there had been a revolution. Everything was turned upside down and it was an indescribable mess. Mother asked resentfully where I had been and what I had been doing the whole time, instead of helping. I hurriedly told her what I had heard, that there was apparently going to be a deportation from the ghetto the next day. As always, we had no idea what to do.

The next day, Sunday, we learned that registration was going to take place on Jozefinska Street. Everyone who had a *Kennkarte* was supposed to report there and they would supposedly get some sort of stamp. Mother, Father and I went there and stood for several hours in a crowd, in unbearable heat. All of this with Father's health! We finally got into the building and people were sent alphabetically to different tables where Gestapo officials sat. We approached one of them. Father put his *Kennkarte* and mine down on the table. The official looked Father up and down with the sort of gaze that gives you goose bumps, then immediately stamped his *Kennkarte*, uttering only one mysterious word: *"Glasermeister"* [master glazier]. Then he stamped mine and we walked away. We were lucky. We did not know exactly why, but we were.

Uncle Szymek and my aunt didn't get stamps. Nothing could be done. Uncle Wicek and Aunt Fanka had the same misfortune.

The rest of the day was spent discovering who had got a stamp and who hadn't.

Uncle Szymek woke us up on Monday morning to tell us that they had taken Aunt Fanka away at night and that she was in the Optima yard,[59] with all the deportees. So it was. Everyone without a stamp was to be deported. The Jewish community had a contingent allotted for each day, so the OD was going through the buildings and taking people. They took Aunt Fanka. They had to leave Uncle Wicek because he could not walk. They began taking those people to Zgoda Square[60] that morning, and from there transported them by truck to the train. That was when we said our final farewell to my aunt. As for Uncle Wicek – words fail me.

We thought that things had ended for the day and Father and I even wanted to go to town, but they would not let us out. Then, right after dinner, German police and SS blocked our street and the ones nearby. I was alone at home with Janek, since Mother and Father had gone to see Uncle Wicek. I did not know what to do because I had a stamp, but Janek was entered on Father's *Kennkarte* and had nothing. I was in despair. Janek and I divided up the money between us and waited. We could hear shouting and weeping from the street. I went to the window and saw the SS herding people like cattle, kicking and beating the defenceless people with their rifle butts. It was a terrible sight. I could not watch, so I backed away. A moment later, the Germans came to our apartment. We were ready for everything; nothing mattered to me any more and Janek had also stopped crying. One officer came in and looked around. I simply don't know how I managed to explain our situation so fluently and the fact that we were alone, but he understood at once and left politely. A stone was removed from our hearts. Now we realised how great is a person's desire to live. We were egoists, the way we experienced it all. The end came after more or less an hour. Mother and Father rushed in filled with dread about what had happened, but everything was alright. The woman and the little girl who had been with us two days earlier had been deported. People's fates depended on whether they were lucky or not. That was how we all saw it.

The building where Uncle Szymek lived had not been searched for the time being, so there was nothing new there. Uncle Szymek was trying to find some sort of job. My father also asked several of his acquaintances, but nothing could be done.

The ghetto was still surrounded. To get to Kingi Street, we could only go by way of Podgorze Square because the other gates were closed. Since our route around the ghetto was full of the *Sonderdienst*, who harassed every Jew they met, we went several kilometres out of our way to avoid being harrassed.

THE DIARY

Tuesday and Wednesday passed peacefully. Then on Friday, everyone was summoned to report for work outside the *Arbeitsamt*. When we left home, there were already SS everywhere, roaming the streets and beginning to surround the buildings that had not yet been searched. We stood for hours and then returned home after seeing that it was pointless. Several hours later, after finishing their 'honourable' job, the SS and police again left the district. Another three thousand or so people were deported, among them Uncle Szymek and my aunt. Poor Edek and Lusia were left alone. What could they do alone? What a terrible fate we had, and to think it was all happening in the Twentieth Century and being done by people with a centuries-old culture! Children without parents, mothers separated from them and transported into the unknown. That was nothing. People who could not walk fast enough were simply shot. They shot them like defenceless rabbits, what did one bullet more or less matter? The main thing was to acquire skill in that trade. That day, about 100 such incidents were counted. And the sick, who were unable to walk, were carried on stretchers to the trucks and thrown inside like sardines; no one cared whether they got there dead or alive. In general, people were treated like cattle.

The *Sonderdienst* still stood all around the ghetto, and in their boredom they practised throwing stones at window-panes or shooting at windows. A very pleasant game.

On Saturday they were registering once again, checking stamps and giving out blue cards for permission to live in the ghetto. We got one so once again we were lucky, but no one could feel secure after seeing what was going on all around. People who did not get cards were taken immediately to Optima with nothing, as they stood there. Then they robbed them of their money and everything they had. Those families were supposed to go there on their own at noon on Sunday. Afterwards, everything was to be checked, and then it would be just like the previous days, and several thousand more people would disappear into the unknown. Yet those who were wise avoided this.

Throughout this operation, we all went around as if we were hypnotized, doing whatever we were ordered to do. On top of everything else, the rumours magnified everything and made people very nervous.

THE DIARY

Among the things I have not mentioned, I should add that this was when, for the first time in my life, I saw people who had been killed or beaten. One such incident happened in our street. In a courtyard lay a poor man who had apparently been shot because he could not run fast enough. The sight made a great impression on me and I could not get it out of my mind. A second similar incident happened when I went to our workshop two days after the deportation. A few moments after I got there, I heard movement in a nearby yard. I went out and saw that a Jewish hearse had driven up and the gravediggers were starting to dig in the ground at a spot pointed out to them. I went closer and learned that two people who had been shot in the street were supposedly buried there. Because it was impossible to take them to the cemetery, everyone in the building had been ordered to come out and dig a grave to bury them there. The work was taking a long time, so I helped them. I wanted to see the result. After about half an hour, what can I say, we dug out two corpses, a woman and a man, in the first stages of decomposition. For several days, I was ill whenever I thought about it and I kept seeing it before my eyes. Those days were nerve-racking and took a toll on our health, but what could we do, living in those circumstances? I cannot even count all the similar cases of barbarism and savagery. Perhaps some day there will be a better occasion to do so. But the most important thing, which I have neglected to mention so far, is that the collection of the deportees' property began while the operation was still going on. The Germans had the 'Polish Construction Service' (very good thieves) to help them. They drove in trucks around all the apartments and sought out whatever could be taken away. The furniture was taken to a building at 4 Limanowskiego Street,[61] and the clothing and linen to the school at 60 Limanowskiego.[62] That was the beginning of my future workplace.

A few days later, an order was issued for the reduction of the ghetto by about half its former extent. This was a great deal, since a quarter of the people had been resettled. Yet there was no way around it. We lived in the unlucky part and suddenly had to begin searching for an apartment – in vain, since everything had been taken and we were left out in the cold. As the deadline drew near, we still had nothing so we had no choice but to begin moving our things to the workshop on Jozefinska Street. Then came the fatal day. People with nowhere to live – and there were several hundred of them – were sleeping outdoors. We were in the workshop. I intended to throw out various articles we did not need and convert it into an apartment. And then the next day, for a reason I cannot guess, a new ruling came out, that people who still did not have anywhere to live were to move immediately, that same day, to the block of houses on the other side of Lwowska Street, which had been re-assigned to the ghetto. Those houses would later be known as 'the Ukraine'. They were fenced off separately with barbed wire so you had to cross Lwowska Street, through two checkpoints guarded by the police, to get to them. That was how things stood: the ghetto was divided into two parts. We immediately looked for an apartment and managed to find one that had belonged to a woman we knew at 5 Dabrowki Street. A caravan of people formed. In one direction there was a line of people loaded down with their possessions and in the other, people hurrying back to get more goods. It was all a great rush since everything was supposed to be finished by nine o'clock in the evening. We barely managed on time. Once again we had found a new apartment and I had carried everything. I was very tired and sleepy, so I lay down without even undressing. That was the beginning of our residence in 'the Ukraine'. As usual we had to give notification of our address and there was even more registering to do. A person never had any peace.

I carried on working with Father, either at building sites or at home. Every occupation was organized into a *Gemeinschaft*,[63] and we were in the construction *Gemeinschaft*. Later, we were transferred to a newly established workplace that restored furniture for the SS. We had to put glass in various pieces of furniture. That was the beginning of the job that I have been doing ever since. At first we only went occasionally because there wasn't much to do, so I also worked at a factory in Zablocie[64] that made pots and pans.

So the summer months passed. We lived from day to day. Prices were going up and up and it was getting harder to do anything. How can you live on one loaf of bread a week? That works out at 100 grammes per day. Then there would be a few hundred grammes of coffee or sugar per month, and it was forbidden on pain of fines or imprisonment to trade on the black market. Yet no one wanted to take notice of this and everything went on as before.

There was commotion at the *Arbeitsamt* with regard to people's assignments. People lost their jobs and were given other assignments. Going out on an individual *Passier* was no longer allowed, only groups of five. In general there were great changes, all intended to make things difficult for people.

We learned from the newspapers that the Germans had got as far as the Caucasus on their southern front and had even reached Stalingrad, which they were fighting for. We predicted, however, that they would not take it, despite the statements in the press and various declarations by German leaders.

In view of the ever-increasing difficulties, you had to fight with everyone. There were various complications with my job, as a result of which Father and I were dismissed. I returned a week later. Although Father could have done the same himself, he resigned. Some time later, it became clear what a mistake this was. Life went on in a monotonous circle, getting worse and worse.

For several nights, we were woken up by air-raid alerts. We listened to the prolonged screeching of the sirens, which reminded us of the distant beginnings of this long war. In the night-time silence, we could also hear the far-away sound of aeroplanes flying somewhere very high. How lovely it was to be reminded that those harbingers of freedom were so close to us, as if they had come so we would not lose the hope of seeing the dawn on the horizon someday. Various hypotheses circulated about how they could do it and from how far they had flown. Our optimism increased by the moment.

Now, however, for something about my own affairs. I was working continually at 4 Limanowskiego Street. My job was not very difficult since I was working in my own trade. Father then began making a little money and our circumstances improved somewhat, but not for long. Then came the deportations from Wieliczka[65] and that city was made *Judenfrei*. This reminded us again of those days in June, which in turn brought to mind our relatives about whom we had still had no news. With the deportation from Wieliczka, we lost Aunt Lorka and Fela, who had gone there from Lwow, as well as many distant relatives and acquaintances. We heard terrifying news about incidents of mass butchery in the Niepolomicki Forest[66] and in Wieliczka itself. Some time after that deportation, we received large amounts of furniture in very good condition: it was the property of unfortunate people who were somewhere and did not even have a slice of bread. Some of those present at that transport managed to line their pockets and made many thousands, but they were isolated cases. In general, things were more and more difficult; everything was more expensive and you had to sell a great deal to support yourself in a very modest way.

In September, events again took an unsettling turn and there was continual talk of deportation. No one knew anything precise. They said that all the ill, elderly and children would be deported, or all those over sixty, even if they had a blue card, or only the sick who did not have a blue card with a *kopfzetl*[67] – and everything got all mixed together and blown out of proportion, which caused a veritable storm of rumours in various versions. This was hardly strange in view of the news arriving from other cities, for instance, that they had deported everyone who was found at home, whether they were working or not. When somebody said that all the children had been deported from Rzeszow,[68] it was enough to send you into black despair at the very thought of it, not to mention the people of whom there was no news. I don't know how people were able to know the date of future deportations, whether they were really so well informed or not. We knew too much about everything. The worry was enormous. People tried to protect themselves as best they could, either by escaping from the ghetto or spending many thousands to obtain a work assignment. One of the dates that people talked about was right before the Jewish New Year holidays. Everything was prepared, and then there was a general relaxation and it seemed the deportation had been postponed for a month. People's expressions improved, since it seemed like the postponement of a death sentence, and that meant a lot. The holidays passed relatively peacefully and, as far as was possible, even solemnly. Yet we still had to go to work. I remember that when I went to the prayer house on the evening before Yom Kippur, the mood was truly solemn and uplifting. Given the current situation, I doubt if anyone stayed at home. Everyone wept after the singing of the *Kol Nidre*; there was no one with dry eyes and on every face there was emotion and a silent plea for a rapid end to our misery.

THE DIARY

My father had been sick for some time. At the beginning, w e did not know exactly what was wrong with him, whether he had an obstruction, since he went constantly to the toilet but was continually constipated and unable to move his bowels, or whether it was something else. We were somewhat sceptical about it all, but his constantly deteriorating appearance and continual weight loss forced us to seek medical advice. Without telling Father, Mother informed me that Father had an ulcer in his colon and must undergo an immediate operation. This came as a great blow to us since an operation and illness were risky business in those uncertain times. We did not know what to do and no one could advise us. We did not have the money for the surgery so we had to try to sell something. We intended to sell two motors to raise the necessary cash. All of this, however, slowed down matters that were urgent. I don't know whether or not the operation was dangerous; in any case, it was hard for us to decide.

One day, we suddenly learned that people in our district were to move to the other part of the ghetto by nine o'clock that evening. This brought us back to reality and we hastily began packing whatever we could. Then, several hours later, the move was called off. I don't know how this happened, but for the time being we were staying. However, it did not last long because it all happened again a few days later, without an official edict this time. It made no difference to us because, as they said, it would be forbidden to take anything along, so we moved everything we could to the workshop on Jozefinska Street instead of waiting. At the one checkpoint there was indescribable crowding, made worse by the OD who did not want to let people through because no decree had been issued. Mr. Kudla, the head of a shop similar to the one I worked in, took advantage of this by passing among the people and taking from them what he could. My dear mother and father were among them; he took clothing, an overcoat, two dresses and a lady's suit from them. We did not know what to do. We pleaded and begged, but nothing helped. He took those items to OD headquarters and locked them up there. In the meantime, it all turned out to be unnecessary since there was no need to move at all.

Once again, there was talk of imminent deportation. The things we lost could have been sold for the money that we so badly needed at that time. All our efforts went for nothing.

Yet this was nothing. The tension rose and the constant presence of the authorities in the ghetto was upsetting. All of it, however, was leading up to the deportation about which there had been so much talk and speculation.

The deportation happened on 28 October and it was the greatest blow to me in my life. Coming home from work the day before, I noticed a tremendous amount of traffic at the checkpoint. People were fleeing *en masse* from the ghetto and above all taking their children out. Something was hanging in the air. Everyone knew that something was going to happen, but no one knew who would be affected. That was why people without permits for their children and old people were escaping from the ghetto, because they were most at risk. This was not the case for us since Father and I had secure jobs and Mother did sewing at home (mending uniforms). My brother was also safe. He worked in a carpentry shop even though he was not yet fourteen, and had received a *Meldekarte*[69] with a stamp, the equivalent of a blue card, a few weeks earlier. But we did not know what to do with Uncle Wicek, who was living with us. A cripple, he could not move about or be hidden or taken out of the ghetto: we were truly desperate. All we could do was keep consoling ourselves by repeating that nothing was going to happen. I especially kept repeating that another deportation would be impossible. An evening came when the *Sonderdienst* surrounded the ghetto without our even knowing how, and the OD declared a state of strict readiness. We went to bed very late, having spent all our time listening to fairytales and various rumours. We were awakened during the night by the sound of weeping from the other side of the wall. We learned that our neighbour's wife was in the hospital and he had been informed that the entire hospital was to be emptied (which meant, as I later learned, that as in the previous deportation, the Germans had already loaded all the patients into trucks and taken them away somewhere).

Something was certainly beginning. The *Ordnungsdienst* were supposedly going around with a list (from the *Arbeitsamt*) and collecting people to make up the contingent specified by the authorities. This was just the beginning. They sent these people to Zgoda Square where the Germans were waiting. I believe it was at five o'clock in the morning that we found out that everyone with a work assignment had to be at the *Arbeitsamt* by seven, and from there they would go to work. I guessed that in the meantime, while we were on Jozefinska Street, they would search the buildings for everyone who was left, and that would be the end of it. Acting on this assumption, we did not prepare at all. Mother and Father did not even take any warm clothing, just old clothes so it would look as if we were going to work. Only Uncle Wicek remained behind in bed and it was heartbreaking to think what lay ahead for him. He had already prepared himself for any eventuality, but what could we do? Our hands were tied. We went out on the street when it was still completely dark and by the light of the lamps we could see that a great crowd of people was waiting to be let through at the checkpoint from our part of the ghetto.

I couldn't understand why we were supposed to be at the Arbeitsamt at seven o'clock, since they were not yet letting people through. What could we do? We all joined that crowd together so as not to get lost; so that at least the fate of one would be the fate of all. It was almost seven when they opened the gate and a German policeman began letting people through in small groups to avoid a stampede. As fate would have it, as it later turned out, Father was standing just in front of us and was let through in the group before; then they cut us off from him. Father acted as if he were still asleep and did not even hear my call to stop. That was the last time I saw my father, since he turned around again and smiled at us in a strange way. Janek started crying and I soothed him as best I could. I no longer recall everything I said or how I consoled my mother and brother. The next group was let through several minutes later and we stuck together. When we got to the other side, we were seized with panic and everyone started running because it was already past seven. We too were caught up in that frenzy and began to hurry.

Passing near the workshop and seeing what was happening all around us, I decided, just in case, to lock Mother in there so that she could hide until it was all over. Without thinking too much about it, I put the plan into action and ordered her to stay under the table and not give any sign to anyone that she was there. That was the last time that I saw and said farewell to Mother, yet I did not know that it would turn out that way. And then I had more bad luck. I looked everywhere but Janek was gone. Alas, how difficult it is for me to write this! My poor brother was caught up in the panic and did not wait for me; he must have run along by himself, and where on earth could I look for him among these thousands of people? I started searching. Oh, how I longed to find Father and Janek. I passed near the branch of our shop at 31 Jozefinska Street. I thought that, as a last resort, I could go to work or hide there. With that in mind, I kept running. I looked in every direction and saw various Germans using whips to chase people, or to break up groups who had no idea where they were supposed to go. I was in the same predicament as everyone else and did not know what to do with myself.

There was great confusion in the street. I turned back and went to that building. What would be, would be, and it was all the same to me. I only wanted it to end so that we could all be together again. Hour after hour passed and the time crawled along. Our whole shop (all the workers) were brought there from in front of the *Arbeitsamt* and they locked the door. We were closed in and cut off from the world, from our loved ones who perhaps needed help. I didn't know what was happening to Father and Janek. Oh, if only Mother would stay there calmly.

THE DIARY

The German police were going from house to house, chasing all the people into the street and then sending them to Zgoda Square. I could see people trying to hide behind the furniture in the yard of our shop. Our boss did not allow them to do that because it could put us all at risk. A terrible fear overwhelmed people. Mrs. Blonska was with me as well; Edek and Lusia lived with her and I asked her if she had any news of them. Scraps of news reached us from the street. Through a crack in the window, I could observe new developments. I saw the *Ordnungsdienst* lead a whole column of people from the *Arbeitsamt* to the lawn across from our windows, and order them to take their places there. I looked to see if anyone from my family was there. Unfortunately not. I learned later that those people had already been sorted as the ones who were supposed to stay. For the first time, I began to cry spasmodically, as if in presentiment of what awaited me.

There were rumours that the Germans had cancelled the permits of the construction working group. What would become of my father, my beloved, sick father? Would I ever see him again?

The police were still prowling around the buildings and they also came to our shop, shouting for us to come out. It was difficult explaining to them that we had permission to stay there. They left and it seemed again as if a stone had fallen away from all our hearts. What a great desire people have to live, despite seeing all the misfortune around them. Hour after hour passed and we could not find places for ourselves; we all walked around as if in a trance.

At a certain moment, Mr. Frühauf (the boss) came up to me and said he had seen my mother on the street, and she sent her best regards to me. I realized then what had happened to me: a misfortune that is a turning point in one's entire life. I began asking him to let me out. I wanted to save my dearest mother somehow. They did not even want to listen to me. Such heartless people! I later realized that they were not at fault, that they were doing everything under orders. More hours passed: to me they were like whole centuries. It seemed that it was almost over and they were only taking the prisoners from the OD. Some people said it would no longer be permissible to go back to the part of the ghetto where we lived, but no one knew anything precisely. Finally, at six o'clock in the evening, they let us out of the building. We left after being imprisoned all day.

The streets were very empty. A few people ran back and forth looking for their relatives. There was weeping at every step. Oh, God! What lay in store for me now? I ran with a pounding heart to the workshop where I had locked Mother in. Perhaps what Mr. Frühauf had told me was not true. Unfortunately, I found the door forced open and the place empty. My pain cannot be expressed in these simple words. I remember that I came to my senses after a long while, having realized that I had lost my mother forever, without a farewell and without a last embrace. The mother whom no one could replace, no matter how they tried. My beloved mother – she must have wept as she sat there, for I saw the traces of tears on the table. Oh, the thoughts she must have had about us before the same fate caught up with her. (Later, I learned that when the Germans called for people to come out of the buildings, she had gone voluntarily out of fear or blindness, never to return.)

What could I do next except go and see if they would let me return home? But I found out that it would only be possible to remove all my things the next morning. I went back to the workshop because I had nowhere to go. I waited; perhaps Father or Janek would come. I sat there until eight o'clock, but no one came. If my father or brother had been around, they would have come. Where were they now, my loved ones?

I had nothing to do there so I did my best to make the lock fast and went to Lusia's. There were still Germans wandering the streets. Oh God, no vengeance against them would be equal to my misery. And you looked on and permitted it to happen, God. It was surely not the time to blaspheme, but the sorrow that tore at my lips could not be assuaged. I needed something more, something that in any case was then out of reach.

I will never forget the warmth with which Lusia greeted and consoled me. She and Edek had been left behind. They were now the only loved ones with whom I could cry my eyes out. I could write much more about the events of that evening, but it would be more or less boring. I will only add that I spent the night in continual weeping and torment. Another cousin, Julek, also moved in with us.

First thing the next morning, we all hurried to my apartment to rescue the things that had been left there. We found the door broken down and the apartment empty. Uncle Wicek was gone. Who knows where they had taken him since he was incapable of moving on his own, or whether he was even alive? Somehow, we got through such awful moments and got used to them. We took everything but the furniture to our workshop since that part of the ghetto was supposed to be completely vacated by twelve o'clock. I was running on my nerves alone, with no tiredness, without eating or drinking anything. At nine o'clock, I noticed a great commotion in front of the OD. I could see that several *Ordnungsdienste*[70] seated in *dorozki* were being showered with pieces of paper bearing names and requests that people be rescued from the transport, which was supposedly still in Plaszow.[71] I was among them, but I could not push through to hand them my paper. Yet perhaps there was still something I could do.

A plan came into my head. I could run to the station on my own and perhaps see them, even if it was for the last time. I quickly gathered up whatever warm things of theirs were at hand, like caps, scarves, and gloves, and ran to the gate. I had a hard time getting through, pretending to be on my way to work with some important business to take care of. I did not care about the risk involved in running as far as Prokocim. I ran all the way without stopping, not even feeling tired and with one thought and hope – to see them or help in some way. *Dorozki* full of *Ordnungsdienste* raced along the road, and everything I felt was full of the hope of seeing my beloved ones. What a disappointment I felt when I reached the place and learned that the transport had departed long ago. I lost my last hope of offering any kind of help, my last hope of even being able to wish them well. All at once I had lost everyone, everyone who was dear to me, and only later did I understand this. How difficult it was to get used to my emptiness and loneliness. But this was obviously fate's punishment for me and there was no way I could stand up to it. In those sad moments, I was supported by the will to survive all our misfortunes and, if a happy ending brought me out of it successfully, perhaps to help my loved ones, whom I might yet see again, and to soothe my pain.

I will add that on my way back from Prokocim, I dropped in on various acquaintances from Kingi Street and poured out all my despair to them. They comforted me as well as they could and told me various details I had not known about. They had seen all of them. Father went in the second transport and Mother and Janek in the third, but separately. My poor father managed to say goodbye to all of them and held his hands out helplessly to show that he was going into the unknown wearing a summer coat and street shoes. Dear Janek wept terribly as he walked alone. Perhaps he met up with Mother somewhere because they were not far from each other.

Oh, God! Who could say what awaited them, what new misery lay ahead as they walked into such a horrible winter completely unprepared? I still had constant contact with my acquaintances from Kingi Street, since the one thing my father left behind was a great many people he knew who were loyal and good-hearted and were familiar with the meaning of pain and despair.

A new life began for me in which I had to show more independence and endurance. Lusia, Edek and I lived together and Julek was also with us. We helped each other, living in constant hope of a better tomorrow.

Now is the time to write something about the news from the outside world that reached us at this time. We learned that the Allies had landed in North Africa and taken the French colonies. This was the first fanfare of our victory. In the other direction, the English were driving the Italians out of Libya and the Russians, beginning their winter offensive, were starting on their plan to defeat the Germans. This news circulated among us with a lightning-like rapidity and we began counting the end by weeks and even days. That is how everything looked. I myself was of a different opinion and did not believe all those stories. Our 'masters' did not permit us to mull over politics for long since that would have been too good for us. The issue of the barracks[72] was emerging and is still going on today.

A month earlier, they had begun building barracks at the Jewish cemetery on Jerozolimska Street.[73] It was not known exactly what purpose they would serve. Some people said they were warehouses, others that they had been requisitioned by the army, and others that they were to be barracks for us since the ghetto was to be liquidated. That threat hung constantly over us, and as before, people again began indicating various deadlines and postponements. The only thing I could not find out was where they got their information from. Step by step, things were being made stricter again. For instance, the *Arbeitsamt* was liquidated and its affairs taken over by Pomorska Street. Leaving the ghetto was permitted at first for five people at a time, then only under escort, and finally in whole groups. Straying from the column or walking alone was punished by death.

Our life became monotonous and began to resemble that of prisoners. You went to work in the morning, stayed there until evening, then went back home and to bed, exhausted, round and round in an unending circle. There were terrible price rises. Everything went up so sharply that a kilogram of butter, for instance, cost around 200 *zloty*, and a kilogram of meat 60 *zloty*. I had to sell things to make ends meet.

And then there was our apartment. There were a total of fifteen people in two rooms. I was sleeping in the first room along with Edek, Lusia, Julek, Mrs. Blonska and her daughter and brother-in-law. We got used to each other at once, as if we were among friends, and we had no disagreements or quarrels. I set up a bunk bed in the room since there wasn't much space, and I slept on top above Edek. This was one of the many pleasant memories from the time of our shared room. In the evenings we played cards or discussed current politics. Then, just when our life seemed routine and peaceful, new rumours and reports upset people, always of the same kind. For some time after the deportation, a certain von Malutki or Vormaluczki,[74] a very degenerate character, had been prowling around. He came to the ghetto from time to time and took several people with him, whether they were off the street or prisoners of the OD. Next, he took them outside town and amused himself by shooting them like rabbits. His terror left a strong mark on us. Various arrests were the order of the day and the prisoners were transported into the unknown.

At the same time, there were more and more incidents of something like sabotage by unknown parties. We did not know if this was a harbinger of the end, or if it was influenced by German setbacks on the front lines.

In consequence, there were various restrictions outside the ghetto: for instance, the curfew was first set at nine o'clock in the evening, and then at six. Some taverns, cafes, and cinemas were closed down.

Our optimism held firm and was reinforced by the progress of the Soviet winter offensive. In the middle of January, however, the question of the barracks re-emerged. Our 'masters' were clearly hurrying to put us in there.

The transfer to the barracks took place in the following way. Early one morning, a given working group would be informed that the following day, following disinfection (delousing), they were to report with necessary personal effects to an assembly point. From there, they would set out for the barracks which were not yet completely ready. It was fortunate that the winter was not particularly harsh that year so things were not so dreadful. However, we were not used to it and so it was not very pleasant for us. I don't remember the exact date when Julek and Wladek A. from our apartment, who worked together, left, or later Edek, Kamil B. and Mila, who all worked at the Zweig company. We prepared them for their new place of residence as well as we could. When the majority of the working groups had been moved there, the operation was suspended for a time. Our apartment became dreadfully empty and spacious. We were not prepared for such peace and quiet and for a time it was terribly unpleasant. I abandoned my bunk bed and slept on a couch.

In the meantime, there were various changes where I worked. Dismissals and fear of such an eventuality, warnings, changes among the bosses, then shipments of new furniture and the hiring of new workers (with powerful friends), and so on.

I have forgotten to mention that there had been a move from America here several weeks earlier. That means that there was supposed to be an opportunity for the exchange of Germans from America for Jews who had the 'affidavit' or entry permit.[75] The possibility of freedom affected us so strongly that people sought various ways of doing something in that line. Those holding affidavits were registered in the Jewish community building. Next, they were all supposed to be isolated for several weeks – and then! Then, the road to freedom, so desired by all of us, might open. My own efforts were made in parallel with those of Liza F., but everything suddenly quietened down several days later and people from Bochnia, who had come for that quarantine period, went home. In Krakow, too, people slowly stopped talking about it. Something had obviously gone wrong and all our plans amounted to nothing.

THE DIARY

And now I have reached the present. I don't know how I have managed to remember everything, perhaps not so accurately or in detail, but my only excuse is that I am writing a description of this kind for the first time in my life, with no idea of how to go about it, and so much time has passed and so much has happened that some things have been pushed out of my head and memory. I have been thinking for a long time about how I should write now. Should I keep a sort of diary, or perhaps report every so often on everything that has happened? In any case, it will be a bit more precise, since I shall be taking the description straight from life.

As luck would have it, I have again fallen behind in my writing. I have been lying in bed for three days for the simple reason that I don't feel very well, having fallen ill with chills and a fever. It's common influenza and the second day I had a high fever and terrible aches in my legs, my head felt unnecessarily heavy and in general I felt terrible. It seems I have even been crying, not from the pain – or only a bit, but rather because various thoughts keep coming into my head about my dear ones, who have been gone for more than four months, and without whom I feel very bad. Dear Lusia is taking good care of me and trying her best. Oh, she is so miserable herself now! Edek comes from the barracks every day with worse and worse news, which I shall write down from the beginning.

For some time, the commandant in the barracks was Müller,[76] but his place was taken three weeks ago by Mr. Goeth.[77] He is a horrible man, but more about that later. As a penalty, everyone from the *Luftgau*[78] was sent to the *Barakenbau*[79] there several days ago. The women were forced to move earth in wheelbarrows and every step of the way they were hit with a stick. The penalty for the smallest infraction was 25-50 lashes.

Unable to stand such work, several women escaped somehow and this was discovered. Mr. Goeth was furious and ordered that six OD-men be locked up until the fugitives were caught. He threatened them with the death penalty. The ghetto was turned upside down day and night looking for them and they managed to catch two girls. Under an escort of perhaps twenty men, they were led to the barracks. We did not know exactly what was in store for them; we thought they would get a beating and that would be the end of it. It was only in the evening when our people were due back that we learned that those two women were to be hanged at seven o'clock. We never realized that such a thing could happen. Perhaps it is untrue and just another of those rumours that is put out. Everybody was concerned about it. In the evening and all day the only talk is of the barracks. The harshness there is incredible. I will give a couple of examples: for instance, washing is forbidden but you have to be clean. Heating, boiling or washing anything is forbidden, yet you have to walk around in clean clothes. You are not allowed to have a chamber pot or any other vessel in the barracks at night and it is also forbidden to go to the toilet; so the thing to do would be to go under the mattress, but that would harm the person lying below. For the slightest bit of dust, the penalty is a beating with a riding crop on the bare behind. Supervision, inspection and searches all night, and the stick they use for beating people reigns supreme over everything.

And Mr. Goeth's orders have indeed been carried out. The hanging of two women – but what women: an eighteen-year-old is still a child – could surely only be done by people with no conscience, by complete degenerates. They were beaten and smeared with iodine all day. They supposedly did not know until the last minute what lay in store for them. When everyone returned from work, the show began. They did not even have rope, so they used ordinary belts. When they had been hanged and were taken down, they were still alive so they were finished off. That such a thing could happen in our times! Even in the Middle Ages it was a rarity, except perhaps in exceptional cases.

11 March 1943

We have had several days of peace and quiet, and what we understand by that is a lack of anything new in our little town. For several days, people have continually been repeating that the question of the barracks is suspended for the time being – until May, it seems. This is allegedly news that came out on the basis of various meetings of the authorities and inspections of the barracks. But there must be something in it since the barracks are again being worked on with amazing speed, and they must be needed by someone. Things have even reached the point where we hear more and more reports that the people from the barracks are to return to the ghetto, and the *Julak*[80] from Plaszow is supposed to go there in their place. We lived in hope of this until yesterday when, like a lightning bolt, the unexpected news came that the entire ghetto is to be liquidated by 18 March and transferred to Jerozolimska Street.

We received this news in various ways. Some people fell into black despair, especially the parents of young children who do not know what to do with them. Others appeal to various examples and assurances and refuse to accept it as the truth.

Optima is to go first. They are to begin going to the barracks tomorrow. If it is true, it is such a surprise as to be almost unthinkable. In view of such news, our working group will also go there for certain at the end of next week.

I am starting to think about my future, about my chances of enduring all this, and in this regard the barracks are not a good omen. I do not know what to choose, the great risk outside the ghetto, or the barracks? There are times when my whole life passes in front of my eyes, before and after the deportation, all my memories of those dearest to me, about whom people say more and more that they are living and working somewhere in the east, and that perhaps they are well off.

This morning I got up and we learned that the deadline for the first shift at Optima has been delayed by 24 hours. It makes me want to laugh. One says this and the other says that: everyone is all mixed up, pure craziness. At home, Lusia has everything packed. As much as possible has to be taken out of the ghetto.

At work, nothing new; half the people are absent. I don't know what to do. Is it time to finish this and hide it, writing the rest on separate pages that can be destroyed at any moment, or to keep writing and hold on to it?

THE DIARY

15 March 1943

I arranged things so that my diary was hidden for four days, and during those four days I could not write anything, and new, unforeseen things happened here. The barracks have become an accomplished fact and Krakow is finally *Judenrein*. When I came home four days ago, Lusia was gone. She was on the list, so she had to move.

We do nothing at work all day long except go to the window every few moments look out to see what's new. A lot is new. Many people are not reporting to Optima; they are escaping or going to Ghetto B for the unemployed instead. There is great despair because 20 hostages have been taken and no one knows if they will be released. It was trumpeted in the evening that all of Optima is to report and there is great panic.

It turned out in the morning that the ghetto was surrounded by German Ukrainians[81] (guards from the barracks), and no one, including us, was allowed to go to work. We did not know what to do; we paced around like simpletons and everyone was very upset. At ten o'clock I went to

Jozefinska 31 to wait for coming events there. For three hours we knew nothing and then at twelve o'clock we learned that all of Ghetto A, that means everybody, had until six o'clock and would be taken to the barracks in groups. There is much to write about this new misfortune. Packing, anxiety, the screams and weeping of abandoned children and mothers, it is all difficult for me to forget. I packed hurriedly, helped others without feeling tired myself, and we put all our things in a separate place at Jozefinska 31, where the whole working brigade was supposed to gather.

More and more panic. People did not even have time to take everything from their homes, fearing that the working group would depart and leave them behind. At three o'clock we were already standing in the street. In my nervousness, I forgot many essential things. We kept on standing there. Our boss, Hasse,[82] came and ordered us to return to 31 and line up there. He himself did not know what to do with us: our foremen asked him to let us continue to live in the ghetto because we are needed here. He thought about it for a long time and finally chose three foremen to stay here and guard things. The rest of us must go to the barracks. In the meantime, I loaded my things onto a cart, hoping they would get there safely. So we went out into the street.

At the corner of Jozefinska Street and Krakusa Street, we were stopped by Mr. Goeth who caught the children and other people in our ranks who wanted to save themselves, and then he beat them and kicked them savagely. We did not know then exactly what lay in store for them and what sort of fate our 'masters' were preparing for them. But what can we do? We are defenceless and must do what they order us to do, accepting everything as being 'for our own good'.

After standing for a long time we finally marched out of the ghetto, which was completely deserted. More and more frequently, we could hear rifle shots aimed at children or old people. We were assigned several *Volga-Deutscher*[83] for the road and it seemed from their own words that they expected us to give them something for escorting us. What a sight it was: a procession walking step by step, like at a funeral, the stares of the Catholics, and many other circumstances. We were almost an hour getting there.

For the first time, I saw the panorama of our future residence, the barbed wire and the guard towers all around, and in the middle the tiny barracks, huddled up against one another, that are supposed to hold the entire ghetto. We had to stand again at the gate and they counted, re-counted, added up and subtracted, and they managed to play around for an hour before deciding that we should go to barrack no. 18. 'At last' we had that life-saving assignment, but in order to get to no. 18, we had to wander around that crowded labyrinth for some time. People were squeezed together, jostling each other, complaining and cursing, not even realizing that it couldn't be helped. In comparison to the others, our barrack is not the worst-looking. It really can hold 150 people in an area of 80 square metres, jammed into three-tiered bunks along the walls and in the middle of the room. The race began to find a tolerable place and co-tenants. I found myself a corner on the third tier, along with Romek L., and we are supposed to sleep together there. Our things are supposedly still in the ghetto and only some of them have been brought here. We run around from barracks to barracks looking for something, but I don't know what. I visit the latrine and kitchen and then I'm back in our barracks. You can get something to eat, a little rotten cabbage and black coffee that is quite bad, and you have to wait in a long line amidst great crowding. When the first night came, it was a lost cause. Despite being exhausted, I somehow found it impossible to sleep on a bare board with no covers. Furthermore, waking up at night because there is supposedly an air raid is no pleasure.

We get up at five in the morning because those are the regulations; we stand outside for an hour because there is a roll-call and counting of people in case someone is missing; and later all the groups which have just arrived from the ghetto, including ours, set out for the roll-call square (the former cemetery, now a flat piece of ground after the demolition of the gravestones which are used for paving the streets and paths between the barracks). There, each work group lines up separately next to a notice board and we wait in the cold wind for four hours while they count us again, look us over, and then let us go back to the barracks. We wander around purposelessly all day among the barracks. I find my belongings on a heap of others, arrange them as well as I can 'at home', and again I go wandering around looking for coffee or cabbage, because I did not bring anything else with me. In the evening there is another roll-call with counting, and then you can go to sleep.

In the meantime, we learn that there was a deportation operation all day long in the ghetto, and everyone who was left there was either deported or shot, most of all children and old people. The number of those shot supposedly amounts to several hundred.

The things that we left behind on Jozefinska Street have been transferred to no. 31 and are being kept there to be given to us later, since other things were requisitioned and taken away, and the people from other work groups have lost everything. It seems that we will go to work tomorrow, but nothing is known for sure. This night, I sleep very well. My two days' exhaustion is catching up with me and I already have a mattress and sheets. In the morning, we are the only group that goes out to work. Oh, what a great relief to leave that filthy place, marked already by so many innocent victims. And what a great relief it is to return to our job, where we would stay forever if they allowed us to. The whole day is taken up by the feverish buying of food since we are all starving, even though we have only been imprisoned here for one day. The ghetto is still in turmoil. All day, the OD lead people out who were in hiding. Several people are hidden at our workplace and we do what we can for them.

We return fairly loaded down with food to the barracks, which we now call 'the hill'. In other words, we say that we are going 'onto the hill' or 'up the hill'. Things are still uncertain. Then another evening and night the same as the ones before, except that in the evening we have a visit from a great figure, Oberführer Scherner[84] himself, accompanied by other rulers of ours. After that, we stand outside again for an hour and freeze until they come and do us the favour of inspecting us.

The day after that and today bring nothing new. We slowly get accustomed to continual roll-calls and counting, except that our life is not yet regulated. We are still lucky that we can wash at our workplace, or wash our clothes and eat dinner cooked by our ladies.

I forgot to write that about two hundred people, caught hiding in the deserted ghetto, were finished off yesterday. 'Finished off' means that they were herded to the cemetery near the barracks. There, they were ordered to strip naked and dig a long ditch, and they were all shot. One more of the many crimes of Mr. Goeth and the others. Today is already 18 March. I am sitting writing all these words that are so painful and unpleasant, that push out from under the pencil.

20 March 1943

It is Saturday. Nothing new for the last two days. We march to work in a long column every day, escorted either by the Polish police or by the Ukrainians. Everything is the same at work. We have frequent visits from Mr. Balb,[85] which means that we have to rush to grab something to work with, and be careful not to be caught washing, doing the laundry or any of the other things we frequently do. It is repeatedly rumoured that we will probably be quartered in one of the buildings in the ghetto. Oh, if only that were true. I don't know if it is really possible, but I hope so very much.

There was a reduction of the workforce at Optima involving 360 women and 80 men, and Lusia was among them. Poor Lusia, what will she do now and how will she manage? They are supposedly going to work inside the camp. What a pleasure. On the way to work this morning, we were stopped near the ghetto by Mr. Haase[86] with his whole entourage and they ordered us to line up. Then we heard a fiery oration about how, exceptionally, no one is allowed to go into the ghetto until two o'clock in the afternoon, and we are all supposed to assemble at our place at 4 Limanowskiego Street. In the meantime, there was an inspection in the ghetto and a search of the buildings to make sure that no one was still hiding there. The day passed and we are once again prepared for the (not very pleasant) trip to our comfortable residence.

21 March 1943

Yesterday afternoon, we had a fairly disagreeable incident in our barracks, and it made an unpleasant impression on me. Lice were found on the clothing and bedding of one boy. I don't know how because I've never seen such a thing in my life. I imagine that all of us could catch them, impossibly crushed together on these bunks. I hope it doesn't happen.

24 March 1943

Four more days have passed and we are vegetating with boredom. From the barracks to work and from work back to the barracks. Every day, we are led under escort like prisoners of war. And every day we walk along that difficult road, after which we are already tired out. The emotions, so to speak, are different at work each day, and each day there is something new.

The ghetto is already being cleaned by the *Sauberungskolonne*[87] and they bring everything to our workplace.

There is a great deal of work. Yesterday I washed several of my things and learned to iron for the first time. I managed somehow.

Yesterday there was yet another hunt for people hiding in the ghetto. Around 100 more people were caught and they were taken somewhere this morning by those Ukrainians (German Russians). I don't know exactly where, but expect to find out this evening at the barracks.

Today I had a newspaper in my hands for the first time in several days. I was cheered by several facts, including that the German counter-attack has basically been halted. There is an Allied offensive in Tunisia, and the newspaper reports that in general there are various arguments among the Allies over the future peace. The fact that they are so certain of victory is something to think about.

I will add that we live in constant fear of a search for money and valuables in the barracks. I have left everything hidden at the workplace.

25 March 1943

What I will write today is not very pleasant because there is talk about yet another crime by our 'master'. On our way back to the barracks yesterday, we learned that the OD had taken people there, segregated the young and old in their accustomed way, and finished them off. But that is nothing. At two o'clock, a general roll-call was summoned of all those who remained in the barracks. Fifty older people were chosen from among them and they too were shot. I need not add anything, since what I have written suffices to give the whole image of this murder of innocent people.

Nothing new with me personally. How I wish I didn't have to write about such things, but what can I do?

THE DIARY

28 March 1943

I haven't written anything for three days because I didn't go to work, and for a serious reason. As I mentioned, we were living in fear of the possibility of a search for money. We kept trying various tactics and ideas so as not to have too much money with us. As luck would have it, I was carrying all my money and my watch when I was returning 'up the hill' two days ago. No one expected any sort of trap since the atmosphere was relatively calm and there were no rumours or stories. When we were already at the gate on the hill, we noticed a strange commotion and various preparations being made by the Ukrainians. I interpreted it as some sort of exercise and nothing else crossed my mind. The strange thing is that as soon as we were inside the barracks, we were swept by various rumours: that there was going to be a search for white bread or they were going to take our money. I broke out in a cold sweat and didn't know what to do with myself, or with what I had with me. People started moving around. The OD was chasing people into the barracks although normally we were allowed to stay outside until 7.30. So it was that after eight o'clock we were sitting locked in the barracks, guarded by two Ukrainians, racking our brains in the greatest anxiety about what would come of this. For safety's sake, I hid 600 *zloty* in the small, attic-like space above my bunk and I made my watch secure by removing a concrete masonry joint from the stove, putting my watch inside, wrapped in string, and covering the hole with cement. Nothing could be seen from above and no one noticed me at work on it. We couldn't sleep, even though I was frightfully tired, and all we could do was listen to reports being brought from other barracks by the OD. The anxiety got worse and there were moments when I regretted that I had put myself at risk. Our 'masters' finally came in at around four in the morning. Strajewski and Janiczek had five Ukrainians with them and they proceeded to shout that we should hand over all our money, gold, silver, foreign currency and valuables. They gave us ten minutes. I gave them 160 *zloty* from among my small change, and that was that. Others gave more or less, according to how much they had and how much they wanted to. A whole chest of money was collected, representing a great fortune. Apart from that, those Ukrainians filled their pockets as well as they could with new watches, money and other items. I forgot to add that we could hear rifle shots all night long and everything was illuminated by spotlights. This was apparently intended to intimidate us and soften us up for what came next. After all this, they made a cursory inspection and left. We lay down temporarily to sleep, but not for long. About fifteen minutes later, they tumbled us out of bed again and Mr. Goeth himself walked in. He spent about five minutes in our barracks because they told him that a search had already been made there. All he said was that we would not be going to work in any case because a search would be made all day and it would be better to hand things in now than to deal with him later. That was all we needed; in itself it was enough to instil in us the greatest fear. I didn't know what to do, so I staked everything on one card and gambled.

Two *Ordnungsdienste* came in at about eight and only made the panic worse. They kept repeating that we should give them everything and avoid bringing misfortune on ourselves, because the Germans would be coming next and we would be decimated if they found anything. Everyone was afraid of everyone else and of being made a victim by the others. People began handing over everything: beautiful gold watches, diamonds, dollars – millions of *zloty* – and I would never have suspected that our barracks held such a fortune.

I was going crazy, but didn't let it show. Twenty of our people were selected to carry out a thorough search and hand over everything. I could see that they would search everything. Not wanting to be present when they found my money in the space above my bunk, I went away for about two hours. When I returned, I learned the whole truth. It was not my money that had been found at all. Instead, they found twenty dollars in gold in my bunk which someone else had put there. I was accused of having left that money there and run away. They searched all my neighbours to make sure they were not carrying anything similar. It was a good thing I was not there: oh, people are foolish and they never even thought that if I had twenty dollars and didn't know what to do with it, I would have put it up above. It was a pity I wasn't one of those carrying out the search. I would have done things a bit differently and found a way to go outside and bury or hide it.

I went around all day terribly upset about whether the search announced so confidently by the *Ordnungsdienst* would take place. Nothing happened, and I only worried now about whether they would light a fire in the stove and whether we would be able to go to work the next day.

So night came and we lay down to sleep totally exhausted. We could hear the sounds of a drunken party from the house where the Germans lived. They could afford it, having collected so many millions in one day. That was not all, because the OD came in – I don't even know what time it was – asking if anyone had a watch and trying to convince someone else to give them something. They would earn the praises of Goeth himself for their dedication and hard work.

In the morning, I could do nothing but take the watch out and put it on my ankle, under my sock, and go happily to work. Everyone envied me, but I would not wish them the time that I had lived through.

29 March 1943

Not one day passes without something new. Another incident happened which was totally different from the preceding ones. When we were supposed to leave work yesterday, it turned out that our foreman T., Mrs. I.K., and Mr. S. were missing. We were puzzled about where they could be. It gradually emerged that Mr. T. had gone somewhere with a German at around four o'clock (he could leave without telling anyone, since he had a key), and Mrs. I.K. and Mr. S. had gone to 60 Limanowskiego Street and disappeared from there, no one knew how. In a word, they had escaped from all the misfortunes we were experiencing. What can I write? We thought there would be big trouble because of this, but nothing has happened so far. It has supposedly all been smoothed over somehow.

I spent the whole night thinking. I am facing a big decision which could be a matter of life or death. It is not easy to pull it all together. I miss direct contact with my acquaintances. I don't know what to do.

1 April 1943

The situation has worsened again. Yesterday a scandal[88] emerged in connection with the escape of a lot of people to Bochnia, and responsibility is being placed on almost all the leadership of the OD and the Jewish community, who have been brought to 'the hill' (they had previously been living in the ghetto). Eventually, they were allowed to go back home in the evening. But that is nothing. During the day, about 100 more people were brought in after being caught hiding in the ghetto and they were joined by people who were hidden outside the ghetto at Madritz's.[89] We knew at once what was in store for them, especially since fresh holes had been dug at the cemetery. All day, we were afraid there would be a search at work, and that one of the people hiding there might be caught.

And what was waiting for us when we got back to the barracks? As soon as we passed through the gate, we heard dull gunshots: the execution of innocent victims. We took a wide detour around that place so as not to see that murder, which looked the same as the previous ones.

No changes in the barracks, nothing improves, we live in gloom and without any future. We now work from seven in the morning until seven in the evening, and perhaps it's better for us that way.

4 April 1943

Yesterday I had a day that might be called full of variety. At around noon it turned out that I had to go to the city by horse-cart to deliver a couch to a certain Mr Anderson. I readily agreed since it had been a long time since I had seen the city. It was Sunday and the streets were so lovely and peaceful; cleanly dressed people were strolling about with no idea of how we are living. Oh, how enviously I looked on all that and how eagerly I would like to mingle in that free crowd. I now realized what a great wealth freedom is. I never appreciated it the way I do now, but what can be done? We obviously committed great wrongs for such punishment to fall upon us. In any case, we took that couch to the other end of town. Mr. Anderson was not happy because a screw was missing. He was very angry and threatened to shoot us all. This made no impression on us, however, since we were used to it. We started back after about an hour and along the way, we were near the castle[90] when a car suddenly drove up and Mr. Goeth got out. You can imagine the impression this made on us. He asked us who we were and where we were going, why and for what, and why there wasn't a guard with us. He asked why we were driving near the castle and whether we knew that we were not allowed to be there. He gave us two minutes to get out of his sight and take the long way around. Driving along Paulinska Street[91] near the Vistula, I noticed out of nowhere that Mrs. P. was at one of the windows. She had not seen me for some three years and didn't know what had become of me and my parents. She called to me to come inside, but I could not go and communicated this to her with a helpless gesture. Then I saw that she was looking for something and handing it to her son, who ran after me and tossed me some bread and put his arms around me and kissed me, calling out to me to endure, to endure this time. Once again, this was one of the many cases in which the people who understood our plight showed us sympathy and helped in any way they could.

THE DIARY

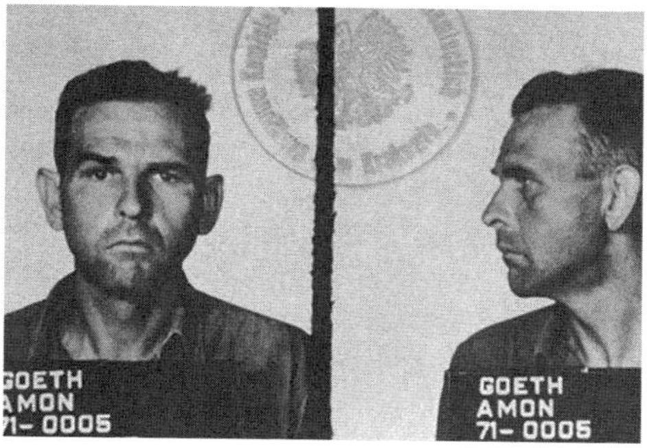

9 April 1943

I cannot go on writing; we are in constant fear of a search for money and clothing; all our clothes were taken from us the day before yesterday. Yesterday we witnessed a hanging and our clothes were painted in yellow stripes to make any kind of escape impossible.[92]

10 April 1943

Today, for the first time, I saw happy Jews.[93] What that means is that these people have foreign papers and are untouchable. Since the resettlement to the barracks, they had been more or less isolated at the OD and today they were set free outside the ghetto. There were about forty of them. Oh, what happy people, being free and able to move about everywhere and not continually having the whip of our persecutor over them. Life goes on normally from day to day, as one might say ironically. We go to work, led there like prisoners of war. But that is nothing. If only that were the worst.

We learn from the newspaper that the offensive in Tunisia is making great progress. Our optimism is undiminished for that reason. They say that some important changes for the better are to be introduced for us 'on the hill'. I doubt it very much. This has never happened yet. But who knows?

11 April 1943

As if in irony at my words of yesterday, on the way back to the barracks we again heard unpleasant news. I don't know where to begin, everything is so complicated. Before we even got there, we learned that there had been another execution. I don't want to write too much about this unpleasant incident so I will be brief. One whole *Barakenbau* group of eighteen people was shot: several unemployed women who could not cope with the stone-breaking work and fifteen people laid off at the Kabel factory. One more crime to match the others.

And where is the Lord God who watches all this and does not help us, who does not send any punishment for these criminals?

Dear Lusia is in complete despair. Working at the stone-breaking group, she saw it all. She has no work assignment and we cannot arrange anything for her since we have no acquaintances. How terribly I feel the lack of my beloved father, whom everyone knew

THE DIARY

THE DIARY

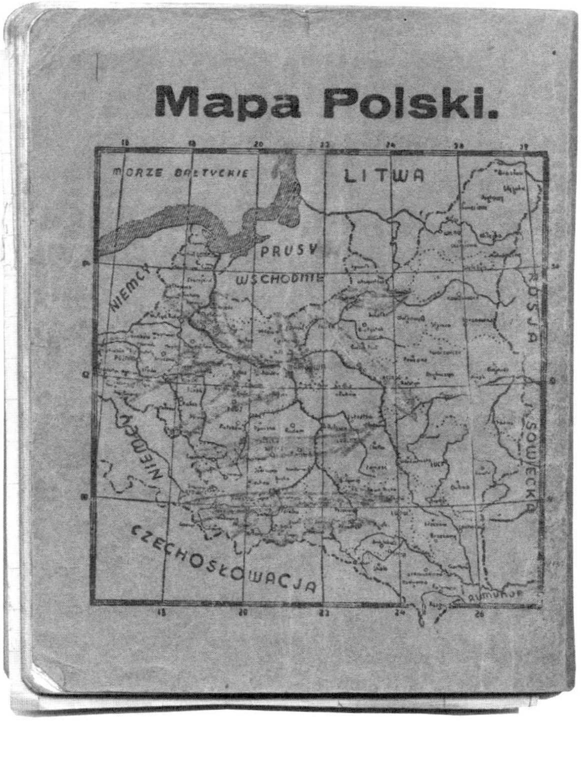
Mapa Polski.
MORZE BAŁTYCKIE
LITWA
PRUSY
WSCHODNIE
NIEMCY
NIEMCY
ROSJA
SOWIECKA
CZECHOSŁOWACJA

PHOTOGRAPHS

Credits

All photographs of Julius Feldman and his diary are published by kind permission of Mrs Gisela Feldman. All other photographs are published courtesy of the United States Holocaust Memorial Museum, Washington, and are in the public domain. The images on pages 11, 25, 29, 39, 41, 47, 65, 71 and 79 are also credited to the Main Commission for the Prosecution of the Crimes against the Polish Nation; those on pages 1, 33, 55 and 61 to the *Archiwum Panstwowe w Krakowie*, and that on page 17 to the *Archiwum Dokumentocji Mechanizney*. For the convenience of those wishing to obtain these images, their USHMM reference numbers are listed below alongside the captions.

Captions

Page ix

A portrait photograph of Julius Feldman, which was stapled to his *Ausweis* (work card).

Page xiii

The first page of Julius Feldman's diary.

Page 1

Jews move their belongings into the Krakow ghetto in horse-drawn wagons, circa 1940. [14692]

Page 11

German soldiers amuse themselves while they force Jews to dig ditches in an empty lot in Krakow, circa 1939 – 1940. [07128]

Page 17
Jews register for identification papers and work permits in the offices of the Jewish Council in the Krakow ghetto, circa 1941. [76087]

Page 25
Jews at forced labour constructing the wall around the Krakow Ghetto, 1941. [39064]

Page 29
View of the arched entrance to the Krakow Ghetto, circa 1940. [73171]

Page 33
A German officer checks the papers of Jews moving into the Krakow Ghetto, circa 1940. [14712]

Page 39
Jewish women are forced to clear snow from the streets of Krakow, circa 1939 – 1940. [07126]

Page 41
A German sets his two dogs upon a Jewish forced labourer, circa 1939 – 1941. [21501]

Page 47
A member of the German police kicks a Jew who is climbing onto the back of a truck during a roundup for forced labour. Two other Germans look on with derision. Circa 1940 – 1941. [73174]

Page 55
A Polish policeman supervises a deportation action in the Krakow Ghetto. Jews, assembled in a courtyard with their bundles, await further instructions. Circa 1942. [50347]

Page 61
After a deportation action in Krakow, a group of Jewish men is assigned the task of clearing out the homes of the deported, circa 1942. [07120]

Page 65
A column of Jews marches through the streets of Krakow during the final liquidation of the ghetto, 1943. [51549]

Page 71
The bodies of sixty Jews from Limanowa, who were executed in the Jewish cemetery, are moved to a burial site. A group of Jewish men wearing armbands pulls a wagon loaded with the corpses along an unpaved path. Circa 1942 – 1943. [18603]

Page 79
A mug shot of Amon Goeth, taken upon his capture, 29 August 1945. Tried by the Polish Supreme Court for mass murder, he was found guilty and executed in Krakow in 1946. [08875]

Page 82
The reverse cover of Julius Feldman's diary, bearing a map of Poland. Note the faint hand-drawn arrows, which appear to suggest the path of the German invasion.

TIMELINE OF THE KRAKOW GHETTO

Compiled by Joseph Soski

1 Sept 1939	The German Army attacks Poland; the Second World War begins.
6 Sept 1939	The German Army occupies Krakow.
17 Sept 1939	The Red Army occupies eastern Poland.
8 & 12 Oct 1939	Hitler makes Krakow the capital city of the newly created General Gouvernement, the German part of occupied Poland. Hans Frank is appointed Governor General, with headquarters at Krakow's Wawel castle.(2)(8)
10 Oct 1939	20 Jews are arrested in the streets and houses around the Royal Hotel and sent to a concentration camp in Germany.(1)
25 Oct 1939	Hans Frank takes over as Governor General.(8)
26 Oct 1939	Hans Frank's first order, establishing forced labour for Jews (*Zwangsarbeitsgruppen*).(2)(4)(8)
6 Nov 1939	Frank orders the deportation of 186 arrested university professors to Auschwitz concentration camp.(1)

8 Nov 1939	SS chief of Jewish affairs, Oberscharführer Paul Siebert, orders all 65,000 Jewish men and women in Krakow, between the ages of 18 and 55, to register with the newly created *Judenrat* (Jewish council), under the leadership of Prof. Mark Bieberstein.(2)(3)(4)
10 Nov 1939	'The Governor General ordered … a marking of Jews is further to be introduced (a white armband with a blue Star of David) and is to be worn by all Jews and Jewesses from the age of 12 upwards. Any contravention of the order must be punished accordingly'. (Hans Frank's diary.)(8)
18 Nov 1939	Otto Waechter, the Krakow District Governor, orders all Jews in his district, starting 1 December 1939, to wear the armband.(3)
23 Nov 1939	Hans Frank makes it compulsory for all the Jews in the General Gouvernement to wear the armband beginning 1 December 1939.(8)
November 1939	On a Monday in the second half of the month, German officers in 17 cars drive through the Jewish district of Kazimierz,

	capturing 17 Jews in the street. They drive to a field outside the city, let the Jews out of the cars, and shouting at them, "Run for your lives", shoot and kill ten of them, wounding the others. (1)
27 Nov 1939	The Jews are ordered to register all mechanical transportation vehicles.(3)
1 Dec 1939	The Jews start to wear the white armband with the blue Star of David.(4)(8)
4 Dec 1939	The Jews must surrender their cars and motorcycles.(3)
3-4 Dec 1939	At 11pm on 3 December a large military group surrounds an entire Jewish suburb around Dietla Parkway and the Vistula river. The Jews are forbidden to leave their houses or even to look out of the windows. The following morning at 8am, all the houses are searched. Officially it is a search for foreign currency, but the Germans confiscate personal belongings and even food. By the time this action ends at 2.30pm, 61 Jews have been killed.(1)
11 Dec 1939	The Jews are forbidden to move from one place to another.(3)

24 Jan 1940	Jews are given until 1 March 1940 to fill out forms declaring all their movable and immovable property. (All property is later confiscated.)(3)(8)
26 Jan 1940	Jews are forbidden to travel by train.(3)
February 1940	Jewish doctors are fired from the *Ubezpieczalnia Spoleczna* (Social medical Insurance).(3)
March 1940	Religious Jews in the Krakow district of Kazimierz cover their beards with cloth, to avoid having them cut by the Nazis. It doesn't help. Jews are often stopped in the streets and the Nazis not only cut their beards, but also their faces. Many are taken to the hospital.(5)
12 April 1940	Hans Frank orders the expulsion of the Krakow Jews, with the exception of 10,000 craftsmen needed by the Germans for work.(8)
1 May 1940	Jews are forbidden to walk the city squares, including the main city square and the *Sukiennice* (Cloth Hall).(3)
18 May 1940	Jews are given three months, until 15 August, to voluntarily move out of Krakow. They are allowed to take their personal belongings with them.(1)(3)

June 1940	The German authorities in Krakow declare that only those Jews whose services could be of use to the Germans would be allowed to live in the city, and all others must leave before 15 August 1940.(1)
Summer 1940	The Germans organize the Jewish *Ordnungdienst*, the Jewish police, under the leadership of Symche Spira. (1)(2)(3)(5)(7)
15 August 1940	In a speech to high placed members of the Nazi party, Governor Frank declares: "The Jews must disappear from Europe." This is printed in the *Krakauer Zeitung*, a Krakow newspaper. By the 15 August deadline, about 30,000 Jews have left Krakow for other towns and cities in the General Gouvernement.
13 Sept 1940	Governor Frank's ordinance restricting the Jews' choice of residence provides a legal basis for the establishment of Jewish districts or ghettos.
October 1940	Another 20,000 Jews are deported from Krakow with permission to take along only 55 pounds of baggage. A total of about 20,000 Jews remain in Krakow, holding special permits.(1)

25 Nov 1940	By order of the District Governor, Dr Otto Waechter, all Jews without permits have to leave Krakow.(1)
December 1940	By the end of 1940, only about 11,000 Jews remain in Krakow.(1)
Jan & Feb 1941	The Germans exchange the *Ausweis* (work ID cards) for the new *Kennkarte*.
27 Feb 1941	District Governor Waechter recalls and cancels all previous *Ausweise*.
3 March 1941	A 13-point order by district Governor Dr Otto Waechter creates the Krakow ghetto in the Podgorze district. By 20 March, all Jews in the city must relocate to the ghetto, and all Poles living there must move to other parts of the city. Responsibility for executing this order is placed on the *Judenrat*. By 20 March, there are about 12,000 Jews with the *Kennkarte* and about 3,000 without in the ghetto, which is surrounded with a two-metre high wall and four entry gates.(1)(3)(4)(6)
15 March 1941	From this date, only Jews with the new *Kennkarte* are allowed to remain in the city.
14 May 1941	Six Jews are executed when Germans discover a secret printing shop publishing underground newspapers.(1)

22 June 1941	Germany invades the Soviet Union.
15 Oct 1941	Jews are forbidden to leave their marked districts on pain of death.(8)
28 Nov 1941	The size of the ghetto is reduced for the first time.
December 1941	Jews must surrender all their furs.
20 Jan 1942	The Wannsee conference rubber-stamps the 'Final Solution' – the mass murder of European Jewry.
March 1942	Jews without steady employment are deported from Krakow.(3)(5)
28 May 1942	The *Aktionen* begin; there is a mass deportation to Belzec extermination camp.(3)(6)(7)
4 June 1942	'Bloody Thursday.' Hundreds are shot to death on the spot. Among them are the folk poet Mordechai Gebirtig and *Judenrat* chairman Dr. Artur Rosenzweig. (3)(6)(7)
6 June 1942	A new ID card (this time called the *Blauschein*) is issued to the survivors of the *Aktionen*.(2)
8 June 1942	An *Aktion* takes place in which about 6,000 Jews are deported to Belzec

	extermination camp. The *Judenrat* is liquidated, to be replaced by a commissariat headed by David Guter. Deportations then stop temporarily.(3)(6)
18 June 1942	At a Government meeting attended by Governor Frank, SS Obergruppenführer Krüger, the Secretary of State for Security, assures the assembled authorities that Gerteis, president of the railways in the General Gouvernement, has promised to provide a sufficient number of wagons to transport the Jews from the ghettos to the extermination camps.(8)
25 June 1942	The size of the Krakow ghetto is reduced for the second time.(3)(4)
June 1942	The Germans establish three labour camps for Jews: *Julag* I in Plaszow *Julag* II in Prokocim and *Julag* III in Biezanow, all around Krakow. (*Julag* is an abbreviation of *Judenlager*, ie. 'Jewish camp'.)(2)
July 1942	After an act of sabotage at the Podgorze-Plaszow railway station in which a train was derailed and one German soldier was killed, the Germans arrest 150 Jews and shoot them dead.(1)

October 1942	The *Zydowska Organizacja Bojowa* (Jewish Fighting Organization) is formed in the Krakow ghetto. Deciding not to prepare for an uprising in the ghetto due to restricted space, they instead concentrate on sabotage actions and attacks on the Nazis outside the ghetto.
27-28 Oct 1942	Another mass deportation. *Obersturmführer* Hasse is in charge. About 6,000 Jews are deported.(2)(3)(6)
November 1942	For the third time, the ghetto is reduced in size.(3) The construction of the Plaszow camp begins near the existing *Julag* I, on the grounds of the Jewish cemeteries, under the supervision of *Oberscharführer* Müller from *Julag* I. (2)(3)
December 1942	The ghetto is divided into two parts, A and B. A is for the employed and B for the unemployed.(2)(3)(6)
24 Dec 1942	Krakow's Jewish Fighting Organisation simultaneously executes several attacks at places often frequented by German officers, including the café 'Esplanada', the movie house 'Scala', the officers club 'Zakopianka' and the officers' casino at the National Museum. Of these, the most successful and famous is on the café

'Cyganeria' near the City Theatre, in which 11 Germans are killed and 13 wounded.(3)(6)(7)

January 1943	The Germans start to move Jews out of the ghetto into the Plaszow camp.(2)
13 Feb 1943	SS *Untersturmführer* Amon Leopold Goeth takes over the command of the Plaszow camp.(2)(3)
13 March 1943	Liquidation of Krakow Ghetto 'A'. About 6,000 people are moved to the Plaszow camp.
14 March 1943	Liquidation of Ghetto 'B'. About 1,500 people are killed on the spot. Only about 75 are selected and sent to Plaszow. About 3,000 people are sent to Auschwitz. Of those, only 484 men and 24 women are selected to remain in the camp. The rest are killed in the gas chambers on arrival. The 484 men are assigned camp numbers 107990-108409 and 108467-108530. The 24 women are assigned camp numbers 38307-38330.(2)(3)(4)(6) That day, several Jews were successful in escaping the ghetto through the city sewers. Among them was Dr. Julian Aleksandrowicz, his wife and son. He was the head of the ghetto hospital at Jozefinska 10.(3)(5)

16 March 1943	Another large transport of Jews goes from Krakow to Auschwitz. Of these, only 15 men and 26 women are selected to remain in the camp. All the others are killed in the gas chambers. The 15 men are assigned numbers 108664-108678 and the women, 38426-38451.(3)
2 August 1943	From Hans Frank's diary entry: 'Here [in Poland] we started with 3,500,000 Jews of whom only a few labour companies are left, perhaps only 100,000. All others have – let us say – emigrated.'(8)
21 Feb 1944	A transport from Plaszow arrives in Auschwitz, the number on board unknown. Only 260 men are selected and sent to the camp, receiving camp numbers 174000-174259. The others are killed in the gas chambers.(3)
24 May 1944	A transport of elderly, the sick and children arrives at Auschwitz from Plaszow. The actual number of those on board is not known. All are killed in the gas chambers.
6 August 1944	A transport of 7,500 women arrives at Auschwitz from Plaszow. They are placed in Birkenau-Durchgang *Lager*. On 23 August 1944, 1,500 of them are selected and sent to the Stutthof camp.(3)

22 Oct 1944	A transport from Plaszow of 2,000 women and only a few men from the camp hospital arrives at Auschwitz. They stay overnight in the camp. The next day, 1,765 women are selected and sent into the camp. The rest are killed.(3)
17 Jan 1945	One day before the liberation of Krakow by the Red Army, a transport of 178 women and two boys arrives at Auschwitz from Plaszow.

Timeline Bibliography

(1) Jacob Apenszlak et al (eds). *The Black Book of Polish Jewry*. Roy Publishers, New York 1946.

(2) Graf, Malvina. *The Krakow Ghetto and Plaszow Camp Remembered*. Florida State University Press, Tallahassee, 1989.

(3) Duda, Eugeniusz. *Krakowskie Judaica* (Polish). Wydawnictwo PTTK 'Kraj', Warsaw, 1991.

(4) Raczka, Jan Wladyslaw. *Krakowski Kazimierz* (Polish). Wydawnictwo Literackie, Krakow, 1982.

(5) Aleksandrowicz, Julian. *Kartki z dziennika Doktora Twardego* (Polish). WL, Krakow 1962.

(6) Israel Gutman (ed). *Encyclopaedia of the Holocaust* (vol.2). Macmillan Publishing, London 1990.

(7) Schneiderman, Sz. L. *Neie Faktn wegn martirdum fun Krokewer ghetto* (Yiddish). Tog-Morgn Journal, 17 September 1956.

(8) Piotrowski, Stanislaw. *Hans Frank's Diary*. Panstwowe Wydawnictwo Naukowe, Warsaw 1961.

(9) Pankiewicz, Tadeusz. *Apetka w gecie Krakowskim* (Polish). Krakow, 1947.

ENDNOTES

1 11 February 1943: If you look at the first page of Julius Feldman's account (see the photograph on page ix), you will see that what he actually wrote was '11 II 1942'. This contradicts the statement that he had 'begun three and a half years late', which would make the year 1943. Other factors indicate that the date entry rather than the statement is mistaken. Firstly, prior to the next date entry (11 March 1943), Feldman refers in the past tense to numerous events which would have been happening at the time. Secondly, while working on his account in the ghetto, Feldman writes only three times more than he manages in one month under the far more difficult conditions of the Plaszow camp. The decision to correct the date in this translation took these considerations into account. Whatever its cause, however, the contradiction remains.

2 Julius' family lived on Kingi Street, in the eastern part of the Podgorze district of Krakow. Podgorze Square, the centre of the working-class district on the right (south) bank of the Vistula, across the river from the Jewish district of Kazimierz, lay about one kilometre west of his home.

3 Born in Galicia in 1867, Professor Ignacy Moscicki came to international prominence as a chemist. A supporter of Jozef Pilsudski, he became Polish President after Pilsudski's coup in 1926. Following the German invasion on 1 September 1939, he fled to Romania with the rest of the government, and died in Switzerland in 1946.

4 The term 'fifth column' was coined by Emilio Mola Vidal, a Nationalist general during the Spanish Civil War (1936-39). As four columns of his army advanced towards Madrid, Vidal referred to militant supporters within the capital as his 'fifth column,' planning to attack the loyalist government from the inside.

5 Szloma and Anda Feldman, also known as Solomon and Anna, lived in the P.K.O. building (Polish Government Savings Bank).

This was one of the most modern and prestigious apartment buildings in the city. Szloma, along with others in the Feldman family, was in the glass business. His store was well known and located in the centre of the city on Sienna street, only one block away from the main Market Square. Their mirror and glass factory was nearby.

After escaping from Krakow, they lived as refugees in the city of Lwow, which was occupied by the Soviet Union. Sometime in 1940, they were deported and forced to settle in a small town in the Ural Mountains. Miraculously, they both survived the war and in 1945 returned to Krakow. Around Christmas 1946 they emigrated to Sheffield, England, to join their only son, Oscar, who had left Poland in 1938 to study in England. In February 1943, Oscar had married Gisela, a Jewish refugee from Berlin who had survived the famous journey on the refugee ship the Saint Louis. In 1949, Szloma and Anda moved to Manchester, where life treated them kindly. Szloma considered those years "the best of his life". He died there in 1963 at the age 79. Anda lived there till 1972, when she passed away at the age of 77. Frydka (Frieda Feldman) was one of the three daughters of Szloma and Zelek's brother David. She survived deportation in the Soviet Union, and married Leon Sternberg. After the war she settled in Israel, where she lives to this day.

6 Bodzow forts: situated along the Vistula river, some five kilometres west of the centre of Krakow.

7 Krzemionki: a hill south of Podgorze.

8 Wieliczka: a town located 15km southeast of Krakow city centre.

9 Warsaw, Modlin, Hel: resistance to the German invasion by Polish regular troops lasted until 27 September in Warsaw, 29 September in Modlin north of Warsaw, and until 2 October on the Hel Peninsula on the Baltic coast.

10 The Soviets invaded Poland from the east on 17 September, under secret provisions of the Ribbentrop-Molotov pact.

11 Dietla Street: the principal avenue on the south side, between the city centre and Kazimierz, which was regarded as the demarcation line between non-Jewish and Jewish Krakow.

12 The resources of the Krakow Jewish community were strained from 1938 onwards by large numbers of refugees from Moravia who fled or were expelled by the Nazis. The Germans established the puppet Protectorate of Bohemia and Moravia in March, 1939.

13 Anti-Jewish regulations: the German civilian administration, established under Governor Hans Frank on 26 October, issued regulations blocking Jewish bank accounts and, on 20 November, forbade Jews to possess more than 2,000 *zloty* in cash. The marking of Jewish shops was mandated on the same day; in fact, the German military authorities had earlier imposed a similar requirement on 8 September.

14 Star of Zion: in Polish as in English, it is usually called the 'Star of David.' The original, however, literally reads 'the Zion star'. It is likely that the narrator was associating the star with its widespread appearance on Zionist collection tins (where funds were collected to support Jewish settlement in Eretz Israel). Such tins were displayed in most Jewish-owned shops, and the symbol was also used on Zionist banners and leaflets before the war.

15 Julius Feldman refers to 'Catholics' ('Katolicy' in Polish) six times and 'Poles' three times. The overwhelming majority of non-Jewish Poles were Catholics, making his use of the term almost as much one of ethnic as religious distinction.

16 A decree of 11 December 1939 banned Jewish education in the General Gouvernement, closing all Jewish schools and expelling Jewish students and teachers from the state schools. Through great efforts, the Jewish Community managed to win permission to re-open Jewish elementary and vocational schools in the autumn of 1940.

17 Commissars: Governor Frank established the *Treuhandstelle* (Trust Office) on 15 December 1939. The Trust Office arranged for trust officers (referred to by the author as 'commissars') to take over local businesses and real estate. Originally this was done on the pretext of ensuring the administration of properties and firms whose owners had fled from the city. Other owners came under increasing pressure to 'voluntarily' accept commissars, who were usually Germans who had

come east in the wake of the army, local Germans who had signed the *Volksliste*, or, especially in Krakow, local Ukrainians.

18 Under the secret terms of the Molotov-Ribbentrop Pact, the Soviets occupied this Polish city (now Lvov in the Ukraine), 300 km east of Krakow, in September 1939. Large numbers of people from Krakow and other places in German-occupied Poland, who fled east at the beginning of the war, were trapped there (although limited opportunities existed for them to return and to communicate with relatives in German-occupied areas).

19 Radio: the German authorities ordered Jews and Poles to surrender their radios on 11 January 1940.

20 On 18 November 1939, the Germans ordered all Jews above the age of twelve to wear the armband. Failure to do so was punishable by death. The Krakow Jewish Community sold and distributed 53,828 such armbands.

21 The Siegfried Line was a 650-kilometre stretch of concrete bunkers, gun emplacements and tank traps forming Nazi Germany's western line of defence. German troops retreating from France in 1944 found the Siegfried Line an effective barrier against the Allies, who did not break through until spring 1945.

22 Pomorska Street: the site of the Gestapo's Krakow headquarters, situated on the north ('better') side of town.

23 Agnysia: an affectionate form of the Polish name Agnieszka ('Agnes'). Before the war, many Jewish and non-Jewish families had a non-Jewish domestic help, often girls from nearby villages.

24 *Arbeitsamt* on Podbrzezie Street: The 'labour office' was originally organized by the Jewish Community in order to meet the collective labour requirements imposed by the Germans. Set up on Podbrzezie Street in the Jewish district of Kazimierz, it was closed in August 1940 when the Germans took direct control of labour affairs, requiring all Jews between the ages of 14 and 60 to register.

25 Sikorski: General Wladyslaw Sikorski, head of the Polish Government in exile.

26 Debica: a small city 100km east of Krakow, containing a large rubber manufacturing plant. Approximately 15,000 Jews were transported from Debica to their deaths at Belzec in July and August 1942.

27 Pychowice, Koszczy: localities a few kilometres west of Krakow.

28 Deportations, Ausweis: Governor Frank wanted to restore Krakow's status as an '*Urdeutsche Stadt*', a historically German city. On 18 May 1940, the occupation authorities announced that Jews should leave Krakow voluntarily until only 15,000 of them remained. If this figure was not reached by 15 August 1940, then there would be forced deportations. An *Ausweis* (a residence permit) was required for those who would stay on. The criteria for granting these permits (which covered employed persons and their families) were vague, the procedure invited corruption, and far more than 15,000 Jews remained in Krakow when the deadline passed. Some reports speak of 30,000 residence permits being issued and of 32,000 Jewish people leaving Krakow in this period. Regardless, the Germans carried out periodic roundups in which Jews were detained at random on the streets and deported, whether they held residence permits or not. Some deportees were sent to nearby forced labour camps; others, transported to the east of Poland, ended up in the Warsaw Ghetto. In January 1941, the German official in charge of the deportation operation was sentenced to eight years' imprisonment for taking a large bribe from Jewish Community leaders (who received lesser sentences).

29 Brzezie: a village some 25 kilometres east of Krakow.

30 Borek: Borek Falecki, a locality some four kilometres to the south, with its own Jewish community. Many people from Krakow resettled there in order to avoid the threat of deportation.

31 Lubicz Street: The assembly point for deportees, near the railway station on the east side of town, was at the Mogilska Fort, at the end of Lubicz Street.

32 Zablocie: an industrial district of Krakow on the right (south) bank of the Vistula, just east of Podgorze.

33 *Zuzug* (literally, 'emigration'): the unofficial campaign, supported by the Jewish Communities of Krakow and the surrounding localities, to resettle Jewish people in suburban localities in order to avoid forced deportation.

34 Tarnowskiego Street: a small street in the Podgorze district, parallel to and around the corner from Kingi Street.

35 Lagiewniki: a suburban district between Borek Falecki and the Podgorze district of Krakow.

36 The *Ausweis* was stamped once for each day of labour. Later, these stamps would be one of the conditions for prolonged permission to reside in Krakow.

37 Retoryka Street: a 'better' street on the west side of town.

38 *Kennkarte*: identification card with a photograph.

39 Lipner: possibly an official of the Craftsmen's Association, which is known to have aided or cooperated with Jewish craftsmen during the war.

40 Lubicz Street: the main office of the *Arbeitsamt*, or labour office.

41 Kalwaryjska Street: a principal street in the Podgorze district, running west from Podgorze Square (outside the area where the ghetto was set up).

42 Zamoyskiego Street: outside the ghetto, in the western part of the Podgorze district.

43 *Passiererlaubnis*: a pass for entering and leaving the ghetto.

44 *Nebenstelle*: branch office; in this case, a branch of the municipal labour office.

45 Deported from Lwow: the Soviet NKVD carried out four large deportations from formerly Polish territory between February 1940 and May 1941. It is estimated that Poles made up two-thirds and Jews one-fifth of the 330,000 to 370,000 deportees. Jews were especially badly affected in the June 1940 deportations. Many who fled east to escape the Nazis died in the Soviet Gulags.

46 Grodek: a town in the mountains some 70 kilometres southeast of Krakow, near the site of several large German construction projects.

47 Franciszkanska Street: police headquarters in central Krakow.

48 *Ordnungsdienst*: the Jewish 'police', an auxiliary force under German control. Feldman uses the term *Ordnungsdienst* (or OD for short) to refer to the organization, its headquarters and its individual members.
49 Szlak Street: the Jewish deportation centre was moved from the Mogilska Fort to 26 Szlak Street, on the north side of town, in February 1941.
50 *Dorozke*: a light, wooden, four-wheeled, horse-drawn cab, usually equipped with a folding hood.
51 OD: the *Ordnungsdienst*, see note 48 above.
52 Micha Pacanowe and his brother Ignacy belonged to the *Ordnungsdienst*.
53 Montelupich prison: the old prison built by the Austrians, on the north side of town. During the German occupation, it held many political prisoners and there were periodic deportations from there to concentration camps.
54 Benedykta Street: in the Krakow ghetto.
55 It was announced on 27 December 1941 that Jews must turn in all fur, ski equipment and ski boots that same day, under pain of immediate execution. Assuming that this material was needed for the Eastern Front, some people deliberately tore their furs into small pieces in order to make them unusable. Eight thousand fur items were turned in that day at four collection points; several people were shot during subsequent searches. Non-Jews were also required to turn in all ski equipment. The Germans may have intended to prevent wintertime escapes over the mountains into Slovakia or Hungary.
56 Grzegorzecka Street: there were German army barracks, military stores and a POW camp for Soviet prisoners on Grzegorzeczka Street.
57 Camps in Plaszow and Prokocim: *Judenlager* I (Jewish Camp—not to be confused with the later, much larger Plaszow camp in which the author was placed in March 1943 along with the rest of the remaining residents of the Krakow ghetto) was a labour camp on Wieliczka Street in Prokocim, two kilometres east of Podgorze. Prisoners from all over Poland worked there for the *Ostbahn* railway district. Some were

engaged in drafting blueprints for the projected Berlin-Baghdad railway. There were also Jewish Camps (*Judenlager* II and III) in Prokocim and Biezanow, the next towns along the railway leading east from Krakow. Conditions in these camps varied, but were not essentially different from those in concentration camps.

58 *Sonderdienst*: an auxiliary police force used in special operations, made up primarily of 'native' Germans employed in Krakow (as opposed to the local *Volksdeutsche* in the *Selbschutz*), and under the command of the General Gouvernement administration.

59 the Optima yard: the former Optima chocolate factory, built by Jewish owners before the war, was turned into a collection of workshops employing ghetto residents. People awaiting deportation were held outdoors in the factory yard between the Krakusa and Wegierska Streets.

60 Zgoda Square: the large square near the eastern end of the ghetto where deportees were assembled before being marched or driven to the cattle wagons at Plaszow railway station. During the large deportations, human lives were bargained for here, 'selections' were carried out and wanton murder committed. '*Zgoda*' means 'concord'; the place is now called 'Heroes of the Ghetto Square'.

61 4 Limanowskiego Street: one of the sites used by the *Zentrale für Handwerkslieferungen* (Central Craft Supply), where Julius Feldman was assigned to work. The German-run *Zentrale* collected, reconditioned and supplied Jewish furniture to Nazi officials.

62 60 Limanowskiego Street: premises used by the *Zentrale*. There were large quantities of medical and dental equipment there, as well as books, some of great value.

63 *Gemeinschaft*: literally 'community', an association of Jewish craftsmen in the ghetto working for German businesses operating on the outside market. The *Gemeinschaft* organizations were used by the General Gouvernement administration as a way of profiting from Jewish labour and by the Jewish Community as a chance of avoiding deportation.

64 a factory in Zablocie that made pots and pans: Oskar Schindler's factory on Lipowa Street.

65 Wieliczka: a town some 15 kilometres southeast of Krakow where, in addition to the local Jewish community, large numbers of deportees from Krakow and Tarnow were held before being transported to the death camps.

66 Niepolomicki Forest: an extensive forest to the east of Wieliczka.

67 *kopfzetl* (or *kopfzettel*): one of the various registration cards required by the German authorities.

68 Rzeszow: 22,000 Jews were deported from Rzeszow (125 kilometres east of Krakow) and 1,300 were shot on the spot in the second half of July 1942. In August, 1,000 Jewish women and children were deported from Rzeszow and murdered at a transit camp.

69 *Meldekarte*: registration card.

70 *Ordnungsdienste* is the German version of the plural. In the original, Feldman actually gives the word a Polish ending, such as '*Ordnungsdienstow*' or '*Ordnungsdienstami*', depending on the tense.

71 still in Plaszow: i.e., still at Plaszow railway station. This transport moved only a few kilometres in the first 24 hours after its occupants were loaded into the cattle wagons.

72 the barracks: i.e., the large camp in Plaszow, then under construction.

73 Jerozolimska Street: leading from Wieliczka Street to two Jewish cemeteries, about one kilometre east of Julius Feldman's family home on Kingi Street. The new Plaszow camp was begun on the grounds of these cemeteries.

74 von Malutki or Vormaluczki: probably Otto von Malotki (or Malotke), director of subdepartment IV-B-5 (national minorities) in the Krakow Gestapo, whose savagery was noted during the June 1942 deportation.

75 Numerous rumours of this sort were current in the ghetto. A later, a similar operation in Warsaw lured Jews out of hiding. The Krakow case may also have involved conflicts between the SS and the Gestapo, and Jews who were at special risk because they had either cooperated

with the Germans or knew too much about the private theft of Jewish property by Nazi officials, or both.

76 Müller: Franz Josef Müller, born in Wiesbaden in 1911, was commandant of Jewish forced labour camps in Bochnia and Plaszow (*Julag* I) and organized several deportations to the death camps; he was also briefly commandant of the new, larger Plaszow camp while it was still under construction. Arrested in West Germany in 1965, he was sentenced to twelve years' imprisonment.

77 Amon Goeth, executed after a trial in Poland in 1946, was feared by the Jews of Krakow even before they became the everyday victims of his savagery as commandant of the Plaszow camp.

78 *Luftgau*: a labour detail.

79 *Barakenbau*: the labour gang employed (at a murderous tempo) in the construction of the new Plaszow camp, at extreme risk from Commandant Goeth's impatience.

80 *Julak*: *Julag*, abbreviation of *Judenlager*, see note 57.

81 German Ukrainians: Ukrainian auxiliaries served as camp guards, among other functions.

82 Hasse: this 'boss' may (or may not) be deputy police and SS commander Willi von Haase, see note 86.

83 *Volga-Deutscher*: ethnic Germans from settlements in southern Russia, 'liberated' during the 1941-1943 German offensive. (As with the plural of *Ordnungsdienst*, Feldman policizes the name in his original, making it '*Wolga-deutscherow*'.)

84 Scherner: Julian Scherner, supreme commander of the SS and police in the Krakow district.

85 Mr. Balb: an SS Untersturmführer, one of those who supervised the disposition of Jewish property left behind in the ghetto after its liquidation.

86 Mr. Haase: Willi von Haase, deputy chief of the SS and police in the Krakow district, who played an especially heartless role in the deportation and liquidation operations. He was tried in Poland after the war.

87 *Sauberungskolonne*: 'cleaning column', the Jewish labourers brought from Plaszow to put the ghetto site in order after its liquidation.

88 a scandal: probably a case (not the only one of its kind) in which Jewish 'officials' were placed in dangerous positions because of conflicts between their German 'protectors'.

89 Madritz's: the military accessories factory owned by the German businessman Julius Madritsch first occupied a building within the ghetto but overlooking Podgorze Square (a location that made it an attractive venue for contacts with the outside world), and was later moved to the Plaszow camp. Madritsch was known for his humane attitude toward his Jewish 'employees'.

90 Wawel Castle, residence of Governor-General Hans Frank.

91 Paulinska Street: a side-street in the 'Christian' part of the Kazimierz district.

92 As also happened in other camps, the Germans made up for the lack of the typical striped camp uniform by daubing paint on prisoners' civilian clothing. Like the shaving of prisoners' heads, this measure was aimed at discouraging escapes.

93 Happy Jews: these may have been the members of the *Ordnungsdienst* and their families who remained on duty in the ghetto after liquidation. The Germans gave them foreign passports and promised to help them escape abroad, but took them all to Plaszow and shot them there on 14 December 1943.